BRAZEN CHARIOTS

*An account of tank
warfare in the Western Desert,
November–December 1941*

by

ROBERT CRISP, D.S.O., M.C.

Foreword by

Field-Marshal Lord Harding, G.C.B., C.B.E.,
D.S.O., M.C.

W. W. Norton & Company
New York London

First American edition 1960
First published as a Norton paperback 2005

Library of Congress Catalog Card No. 60-5845

ISBN 0-393-32712-4 pbk.

W. W. Norton & Company, Inc.
500 Fifth Avenue, New York, N.Y. 10110
www.wwnorton.com

W. W. Norton & Company Ltd.
Castle House, 75/76 Wells Street, London W1T 3QT

1 2 3 4 5 6 7 8 9 0

Contents

CONTENTS

"... Arms on armour clashing bray'd
Horrible discord, and the madding wheels
Of brazen chariots rag'd; dire was the noise
Of conflict!"

MILTON: Paradise Lost, VI, 209

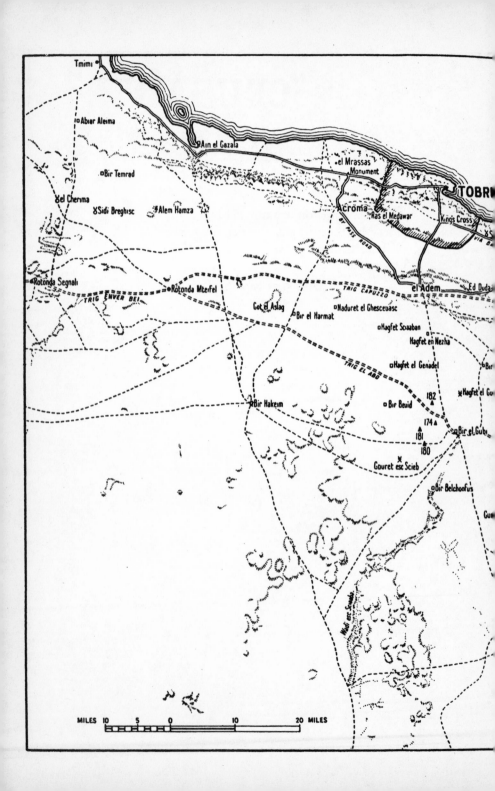

"CRUSADER"
BATTLEGROUND

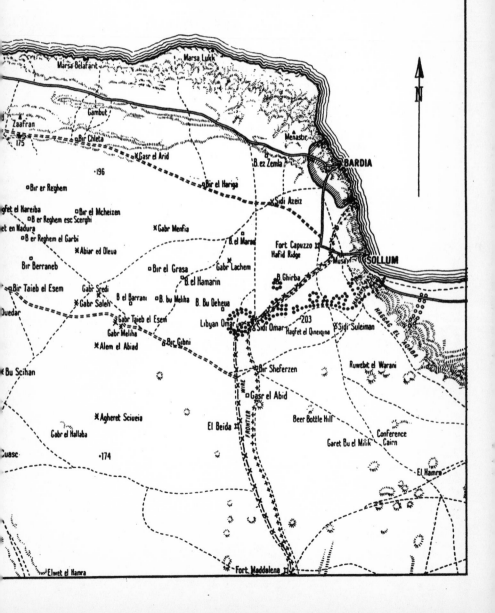

ACKNOWLEDGMENT

The author is indebted to the editors of the official South African history of the Sidi Rezegh Battles for filling in the gaps in his memory.

Foreword

by
Field-Marshal Lord Harding, G.C.B., C.B.E., D.S.O., M.C.

THIS book contains a vivid and stirring story of war—of fighting in tanks against a brave and better-equipped foe in the wide and desolate spaces of the Western Desert. It is the day-by-day story of the life of a man who fought with great courage and daring; a man who knew fear but overcame it, who unhesitatingly put his duty before his own comfort and safety.

Knowing the man and the conditions in which he and his comrades fought—and won—this story rings true to me. It is full of excitement, and full of the agonies and the anxieties of battle.

As I am sure he would be the first to admit, Bob Crisp was not alone in his experiences and achievements. There were others like him—amateur soldiers to start with who made up by their courage and their resolution for their lack of training and their inferior equipment—and for the lack of proper direction too.

This story has a moral for the public and for our leaders today. From all that I have seen of the younger generations since the war, they are not wanting in courage, nor in a sense of duty to their country. Let us hope that the lesson of the dangers of being unprepared that cost us so dear in the early days of both world wars have at last been learnt. This brave story of a little-known part of the Second World War should help to drive it home.

It is for the people of this country and our leaders—political and military—to ensure that if the Bob Crisps of the future have to fight in our defence the dice are loaded in their favour and not against them. Will they? I wonder.

HARDING, F.-M.

28th August 1958

The Days Before

THE Italians were in Sollum; the Afrika Korps and Rommel stood confident and menacing around beleagured Tobruk; The Wire rolled inviolate down the whole length of the Libyan frontier.

In Cairo, the cricket match between Gezira Sporting Club and an England XI was in a very critical state.

I took two wickets in one over, including that of Wally Hammond, and the applause rippled round the khaki-crowded ground. The applause was for me, and I enjoyed it, as I always have done, but it could not drown the sound of distant gunfire.

It was July 1941. Many of the soldiers sitting under the jacaranda trees, spilling over the boundary brown on the green turf, had recently come back from Wavell's brief failure to regain the initiative in the Western Desert. That was Operation Battleaxe, as abortive as it sounded obsolete, and it was allowed to die unsung while the Gezira second innings occupied the headlines in the *Egyptian Gazette*.

On the first day of the previous May I had stumbled off the cargo boat at Port Said with what was left of the 3rd Battalion of the Royal Tank Regiment after the three-months' disaster of Greece and Crete. It was a tank battalion without tanks and without tank crews, an identification number with a few human beings to give it some sort of personality. Then, Egypt and the life-line of the Suez Canal were threatened by a pincer-movement from north and west, and everybody in battledress was utilised in some sort of defensive service, however divorced from original employment or contemplation.

The remnants of 3R.T.R. were not exempt. After seven

days' leave we found ourselves engaged in the local defence of the R.A.F. station at Heliopolis aerodrome, with a stand-to at first light and a stand-to at last light and the intervening day filled with drill and kit inspections and all the ordained occupations for idle hands that seven months in O.C.T.U. had taught me to dislike so much.

Our leisure hours were spent pleasantly enough, sipping tall, cool John Collins' on the paved perimeter of the swimming pool of the Heliopolis Club, eyeing with indecent speculation the cosmopolitan bathing beauties of the region, their figures still trim in youth but burgeoning with discerning plumpness in promise of early seduction. Later, as we got to know our way around, we deserted the unrequited lovelies of Heliopolis and sipped our tall, cool John Collins' around the swimming pool at Gezira, where the only difference was that there was more of everything, and it was not so unrequited.

I was a newly promoted captain. Not for the first time. I had established what must have been a record in swift promotion by being made a captain three months after I had been commissioned in June of the previous year. I owed this entirely to the fact that I had played cricket for South Africa and my commanding officer had once played county cricket for Hampshire. After Dunkirk he had been a bit short of suitable types, and I had found myself making most unexpected holes in my shoulder tabs to accommodate the extra pips. I had no great personal interest in the proceedings, and the situation was speedily rectified as far as the more senior lieutenants were concerned after I had missed the convoy taking the regiment to the Middle East when it called in at Durban. (I had worked in Durban on the Natal *Mercury* for the year before the war started.)

I was in good company—a brigade major, another major, two captains—and we were able to rejoin the convoy only by reason of my friendship with the captain of the cruiser escort whom I had known in his Simon's Town days. By the time we were all back on the troopship somewhere in the Indian Ocean I was 2nd Lieut. Crisp again, with a terrible hang-over from Plymouth gin.

But the Greek adventure had removed two-thirds of the officers, and in the brotherhood of survival it was almost inevitable that Durban should be forgotten and Old Trafford remembered. There were other factors. Down the long, bomb-torn roads of Greece I found I was more reluctant to show my fear than most, and this seemed to be acknowledged by those about me. I think it helped towards my reinstatement as captain; that and the C.O.'s unimpaired fondness for cricket.

Defence duties, training and re-equipping were the banal watchwords of our existence. We forgot them whenever we could at the sporting clubs, at Groppi's, on the roof of the Continental, in Shepheard's bar or Tommy's and, on more opulent evenings, at that huntin'-shootin'-fishin' auberge out on the Mena Road where we occasionally shared the same dance floor with King Farouk. Indeed, on one memorable morning I thumbed a lift into Cairo, considerably after the hours of normal transport and before it was due to start up again, and found myself sitting in the back of a sumptuous sports car with a sumptuous girl in the front alongside the ruler of all Egypt. I have always had a soft spot for Farouk since that night.

It was all very pleasant, and I kept on telling myself that this was the way American millionaires spent a lot of their millions. But the past three months had changed a lot of things for me. One thing I had discovered was that life can be most enjoyable and rewarding in the contemplation of possible death. And I had found out a lot about myself and the people I was fighting the war with. Defence duties, training and re-equipping ... Gezira, cricket, John Collins'. It all contrasted too brazenly with the dark, recent memory of war-ravaged Greece and the noisy desert that waited for us.

I walked off the cricket field that July evening feeling that I had to get out of Cairo. Later that night, drinking beer with some New Zealanders and listening to their stories of adventures deep in enemy territory with the Long Range Desert Group, I thought I had found the answer. Next morning I got off early and went straight to Kasr-el-Nil barracks to see Colonel Prendergast, the youngish tank officer who commanded the L.R.D.G. I told him what I wanted, and he agreed at once to have me transferred to his unit. He said he could more or less ask for anybody he liked, and he would put in an application for me right away. He told me what sort of things I would have to buy, and added that I would probably hear from him in a few days. I walked out elated and went straight to the big N.A.A.F.I. stores further along the river bank and bought myself half-a-dozen shoulder flashes—red L.R.D.G. on a black background. It was all I could do not to tell everybody back at Heliopolis.

Three days later a message arrived at our orderly room for me to call at L.R.D.G. headquarters.

"You're not leaving us, are you, Bob?" the adjutant asked me.

"Not that I know of."

"Want to visit those night spots in Benghazi, eh? Not a chance, cock."

I didn't know whether he knew anything or not, so I kept my mouth shut and went off fearing the worst. The adjutant was right. Colonel Prendergast simply told me that his application for my transfer had been negatived because of the shortage of trained tank crews in the Middle East. No tank personnel could hope to get a transfer to anything or anywhere.

Gone were my dreams of the wide sand-seas of Libya and

the green groves of Cyrenaica running down to the Mediterranean, and the freedom of independent movement far from
brigadiers and colonels and standing orders. It was defence
duties and training for me, with everybody else, and no way
past it.

I went back to Heliopolis unhappy but in the mood to make
the best of it. Fortunately, the tempo of events speeded up
considerably in the next month or two, and we all got a vague
impression of something big being concocted. New men were
arriving every week to replace the losses in Greece, and in
August the first of our new tanks was delivered. We had seen
the sleek, fast Crusader tanks that were going to other
armoured regiments in Egypt at that time, but knew they
were not for us. We were to get an American tank known
officially as the American M3 Light Cavalry Tank—Stuart for
short.

Until then we had been equipped with ancient A10s and
A13s, and even some A9s dragged out of various war museums
and exhibitions. They were ponderous square things, like
mobile pre-fab houses and just about as flimsy. By far their
worst failing was their complete inability to move more than
a mile or two in any sort of heavy going without breaking a
track, or shedding one on a sharp turn.

Of the 60 odd tanks 3R.T.R. had taken to Greece at the
beginning of the year, not half a dozen were casualties of
direct enemy action. All the others had been abandoned with
broken tracks or other mechanical breakdowns. They littered
the passes and defiles of Macedonia and Thessaly, stripped of
their machine-guns, but otherwise intact. They were of no
help to the enemy; no other army would have contemplated
using them. I like to think of them, even now, furnishing
some sort of chilly, overcrowded dwelling place for a family
of homeless Greek peasants.

Whoever was responsible for the design of British tanks in

between the wars ought to have a considerable weight on his conscience. As a matter of fact the design was due not to any one particular individual, but had been conceived by a pressure group, obsessed by an obsolete idea. The principle influence brought to bear on tank design and tactics was the cavalry school of thought. The strategists wanted to make a tank which was as much like a horse as possible, and which could be used in action in more or less the same way. The Charge of the Light Brigade was their idea of the proper way to fight a battle. They merely substituted tanks for horses.

Very unfortunately for the Royal Armoured Corps, the cavalry influence predominated at the War Office before and during the last war (it probably still does) and the fast, lightly-armoured tank was the result. Unfortunately, too, many cavalry regiments employed the same gallant tactics as the Earl of Cardigan. They learnt the hard way.

We regarded the advent of our new tanks with a good deal more vital interest than a newly-married couple inspecting their first home. We were also fascinated by the group of American Army technicians who came with them.

The Stuart was a strange-looking contraption, straight from Texas, tall in the saddle and with the Western flavour accentuated by a couple of Browning machine-guns and the rangy Texans. The main armament was similar to the peashooter that all British tanks carried at that time, but the frontal armour was much thicker than in our own light tanks and cruisers. The really intriguing things about the M3 were its engine and the tracks. Drivers gasped in astonishment when the back covers were lifted off . . . it was simply an aeroplane engine stuck in a tank, with radial cylinders and a fan that looked like a propeller. Fuel was to present a new problem to the supply services, as the engine ran efficiently only on high octane aviation spirit. But this was not our problem, and the consensus of opinion was that anything that was likely to assist in a fast take-off was probably a good thing.

After the engines had received their share of comment, we gave our undivided attention to the tracks. There had never been anything like them in the British Army. Each track link was mounted in solid rubber blocks on which the vehicle moved. After one look we wondered why the hell British tank designers had never thought of it.

As soon as I could, I got my crew into one of the Stuarts and headed out of Heliopolis for the first patch of open, sandy desert—not always as easy to find as you might think. We tested her for speed first, and found that on good going we could get up to 40 m.p.h. It was a comforting thought, in the circumstances, to know that the German Marks III and IV could manage only 20 or so.

Then I told my driver, Whaley, to make a few fast turns, and waited with some foreboding for the inevitable bang-clatter and swerving halt that meant a broken track. Nothing happened. It was wonderful. That tank handled like a well-trained cow-pony.

"Let's see just what it will take," I said down the intercom. "Try and shed one of these tracks."

Whaley put her through a variety of turns and manoeuvres that made the sandy floor of the desert look like an ice-rink after a hockey match, spurting up great fountains of sand and dust behind the tracks.

"That'll do," I shouted to the driver at last. "We're beginning to wear out the desert."

Back at the camp the C.O. and a small crowd were waiting for us. We climbed out, all grinning happily.

"Well, Whaley," I asked my driver, "what do you think of it?"

He, plainly under the influence of the nearby Texan, beamed and said simply: "It's a honey, sir."

From that moment they were never known as anything else.

It was the first practical and beneficial effect of Anglo-American co-operation on land in that theatre of the war, and although the Americans jibbed a bit at the fourteen modifications that our tank experts thought necessary to introduce, it set the atmosphere for the many subsequent occasions when American technicians had to instruct British tank crews in new types of American tanks.

At the end of August, 3R.T.R. moved from Heliopolis to Beni Yusef, some 20 miles the other side of Cairo, where we joined up with the other two armoured units of the 4th Armoured Brigade—the 8th Hussars and 5R.T.R. It was a bleak, hot and dusty place of long tin huts and tents, where we sweltered and swore our way through training and re-equipping, our grunts and groans swelling the raucous chorus from the adjacent Camel Patrol of the Egyptian Army.

My only light relief was provided by my batman's letters to his wife, which I had to censor. He was a holder-upper in civilian life, and wielded his pen like a rivetting hammer with about three words to the page, most of which were abusive references to the "auld-wife". This was a female I could not identify until a visiting officer of the Scots Guards told me it was a mother-in-law. After one spell of about three weeks without a letter home I mentioned to my batman during the course of general conversation that he did not seem to be corresponding with his wife, and I hoped nothing had gone wrong. That afternoon he produced a letter which began: "Dear Wife, I am sorry you have not had my last three letters which were sunk by enemy action. Tell the auld-bitch . . ."

Beni Yusef was a little too remote from the centre of Cairo to get the full flavour of impending events. We heard of

Wavell's dismissal, of course (and were astonished by it), and his replacement by Auchinleck, but we sensed only dimly the new urgency that was creeping into everything. The nearest we got to it, except on our occasional visits to Gezira, was the oft-repeated remark of 'A' Squadron's major, who had been a pre-war subaltern in India under Auchinleck . . . "Bloody good chap, the Auk."

On the whole, we all regarded our removal to Beni Yusef as a piece of typical staff bloody-mindedness.

By the end of September we were a fully-equipped battalion again, with men and machines up to strength. Reorganisation under a new commanding officer, Bunny Ewins, had confirmed me as a captain, second-in-command of 'C' squadron, which meant I kept my troop of Honeys. This suited me fine. I had no ambitions as far as promotion was concerned. I wanted to be left alone to run my troop the way I wanted to run it. The extra money was the only significant feature; I had always found it difficult to reconcile a lieutenant's pay with a major's tastes.

At this time a steady flow of top-ranking brass, including General Cunningham, fresh from his triumphs in East Africa, and—for some curious reason—the Maharajah of Kashmir, began visiting our camp. It all added up to something, and soon we learnt that a great new organisation had been formed with Cunningham in command. They called it the Eighth Army.

It will help in an understanding of subsequent events if I give a brief description of the set-up of 4th Armoured Brigade. It was a comprehensive operational unit composed of the three tank regiments I have referred to, each of which had attached to it a troop of 25-pounder guns of the Royal Horse Artillery, a detachment of the Scots Guards and anti-tank and anti-aircraft units. The whole was commanded by Brigadier Alec Gatehouse, D.S.O., M.C., who could be described as a tank officer as distinct from a cavalry officer, and who was probably the best handler of armour in the desert at the time.

It was the first fully self-contained combat team on such a large scale in the British Army, and I mention it in some detail because it was destined to play such a decisive part in a campaign in which control often evaporated and units disintegrated. Within this entity we were to move and fight, eat and sleep a little, die and nearly die every day and night for the next five weeks.

According to Gatehouse's records, the brigade was in action continuously for the first fourteen days of this period without rest or maintenance, and with an average of two battles a day; the brigade centre line covered 1,700 miles and many unit tanks travelled over 3,000; 172 Honeys were knocked out by the enemy in five weeks (the total strength was 163) and I myself had six tanks knocked out; the average sleep for commanders during the fourteen days was one and a half hours in twenty-four; at the end of the campaign the 400 tanks under Rommel's command had been reduced to 58.

Fortunately for our peace of mind these were events which lay well-concealed and certainly unimagined in the dust and smoke of the future.

The first week in October saw us encamped on the barren spaces west of the Cairo-Fayoum road, for our battle practice with live ammunition.

An inter-troop and inter-squadron competition was arranged to add a little stimulus to the exercise. Troop by troop we went off to the firing area on the wide-open spaces west of the Fayoum Road. I had an idea which I wanted to try out. It was inspired by the fact that enemy anti-tank weapons, especially the newly-introduced 88-mm. gun that had played havoc with our tanks in the ill-fated Battleaxe show, could knock us out at 3,000 yards, whereas the maximum effective range of our 37-mm. and 2-pounder guns was reckoned to be about 1,200. (This turned out to be wildly optimistic.) The result, in simple arithmetic, was that we would have to be within range of their tanks and guns for 1,800 yards before we could hope to get close enough to do any damage. Eighteen hundred yards, in those circumstances, is a long way. It's sixty-four thousand eight hundred inches.

My mind was occupied with two problems: how to get near enough to the enemy, and how to live long enough to get there. Obviously, armour-plating was not enough protection. There were alarming stories going about of what the 88s could do to the massive turrets of the I-tanks, hitherto considered almost impenetrable. The only answer lay in mobility, and pretty fast mobility at that.

At the same time I completely discounted the possibility of shooting accurately from a moving tank, which was what we had all been taught to do when it was not possible to take up a hull-down position. So I worked out a system in my troop whereby, after the target had been indicated, a more or less automatic procedure followed if the circumstances were favourable. The objective was to get close enough to the enemy tank to be able to destroy it. The first order, then, was "Driver advance; flat out". The gunner would do his best to keep the cross-wires of his telescopic sight on the target all the time we were moving. The next order, heard by gunner, driver and loader would be "Driver halt". As soon as the tank stopped and he was on target, the gunner would fire without further command from me. The sound of the shot was the signal for the driver to let in his clutch and be off again. From stop to start it took about four seconds. All I did was to control the movement and direction of the tank.

The battle practice convinced me that I was right, and that in tanks that were outgunned and outarmoured, mobility was an essential element in survival. Needless to say, by "mobility" I did not mean speed in the wrong direction.

I did not win any competitions, but I had established to my own satisfaction that I could get within the effective range of my own gun without the use of concealment and in a fairly aggressive manner. I put myself in the place of a man in the target, and thought it would be very disconcerting to have four tanks thundering down on top of you, all firing accurately and none of them in one position long enough to be aimed at. I was hopeful that by using these tactics whenever the ground permitted, I would very much lessen the chances of being hit. It was not a substitute for the best battle position, which was hull-down upon ground of your own choosing, but I was quite certain that an over-emphasis on the hull-down position in what was going to be a war of considerable movement was not a good thing. It tended to induce in tank commanders a hull-down mind, which was quite likely to develop into a turret-down mind.

By great good fortune, on our return to Beni Yusef from the firing range, I managed to get jaundice, and spent two weeks in the 15th General Hospital, on the Nile opposite Gezira Island, eating boiled chicken and rice and watching the full-sailed dhows go by, while the battalion packed up laboriously and moved on westwards. It was the first major step towards the impending battle, and it took them to the Siwa track, south of Mersa Matruh. That is where I rejoined them.

We were about 90 miles east of The Wire—that fabulous entanglement that snaked rustily all along the border from the coast till it lost itself in the great dunes of the Sand Sea down in the south. It had been built by Mussolini's soldiers years before, to keep out camels and itinerant Arabs who were inclined to regard the Libya-Egyptian frontier as a figment of Il Duce's imagination. Between strong points The Wire was patrolled very occasionally by the Italians on one side and almost constantly by the British on the other. There were some well-established breaches in a continuous state of demolition and repair.

Here, at Abar Kenayis, swarms of R.A.O.C. and R.A.S.C. types descended on our tanks with metal tubing and rolls of hessian. In a few days they had transformed each regiment of tanks into what looked like a convoy of 3-ton lorries. In the dubious interests of security these camouflage devices were known as Sunshields. We were to keep them in position until the order was given "Drop Sunshields", by which time, it was darkly hinted, we would be well inside enemy territory. There is every reason to believe the deception was successful, and that Rommel had no idea that something like 600 tanks had been moved up within striking distance of his forces.

It was in this guise that in the first week in November we moved up to a place called Hallequat, south of the road running between Sidi Barrani and Sollum. This was virtually the forming-up point for the brigade for the attack which everybody knew was now imminent, though nobody knew when or where. From the march to Hallequat there resulted one of those imperial flaps without which no British army has yet succeeded in entering a battle.

The march from Kenayis to Hallequat was made at night, over what proved to be 80 miles of some of the most murderous going in the Western Desert. It was nearly all hard limestone outcrop, but the full extent of the damage to our tanks was not even suspected until daylight, when we had reached our destination. We then saw that the rubber blocks on the tracks of practically every Honey in the brigade had been chewed to bits.

General Gatehouse has since told me what happened when the full extent of this calamity became known. He reported the matter to John Harding (now Field-Marshal Lord Harding) at

Corps Headquarters, and was told to fly to Cairo with Exhibit A and see the Commander-in-Chief. This Gatehouse did, and got an immediate reaction from Auchinleck, who gave orders to strip the tracks off every Honey in rear areas and send them up immediately by rail to 4th Armoured Brigade. The tattered tracks were to be sent back for repair if possible and use on training. He also decided that the brigade should be moved to a more suitable area by transporters. Such was the impetus behind these instructions that everything was carried out and completed in three days.

This was our last but one stopping place before Operation Crusader started, and the last bit of leisure we would have for perfecting our fighting equipment and sending off our final messages of undying love and devotion. Here, too, we learnt for the first time the art of night-leaguering, though it was a familiar enough blackboard diagram. It was a simple and effective manoeuvre for getting all tanks into a compact square, with the thin-skinned vehicles inside, ready to fan out at first light into an offensive formation. We practised it and practised it until we could do it blindfold—which was more or less the way we had to do it in the pitch dark of the desert night after disengagement from battle at last light.

A rather odd thing happened to me at this time. I had been sent out in charge of a small recce party in a 15-cwt. truck to see what the going was like ahead of our area. We had come across a patch of soft sand in which the truck got stuck, and needed a good deal of manhandling to get out. With two or three others I was pushing and heaving at the back of the vehicle, cursing volubly as the wheels spun round kicking up the desert into our eyes and ears, when there was a sudden soft, fluttering noise in my ear, and I felt a light touch on my back.

I took a casual glance from the corner of my eye, and was amazed to see a pigeon sitting on my shoulder. Nobody else

had noticed it, and as I stopped and straightened I put my
hand up slowly expecting any second that the bird would
take fright and fly off again. Instead it seemed to come will-
ingly into my hand, where it snuggled down contentedly.
Only then did I notice the tube of white paper fastened to its
leg by a piece of elastic. I called to the others. They gaped
when they saw what I was holding, and walked back towards
me. I pointed to the piece of paper.

"A carrier pigeon!" said Harry Maegraith. "How the hell
did you get hold of that?"

Maegraith was an Australian troop commander in 'C'
Squadron. We had been in England and Greece together, and
when his ancient tank had broken down somewhere in Macedonia he had jumped on the back of mine with a few other
bods. We were great friends.

While I gently slid the elastic off the pigeon's leg, I told
them what had happened. There was a strange air of unreality about the whole thing which impressed all of us. As
far as I knew we were 10 or 15 miles from the nearest British
formation. There was nothing in sight except sand, rock and
scrub. What was this mysterious paper that had come fluttering down on to my shoulder from an empty sky above an
empty land? A message from some remote patrol lost in the
desert? Could it be a German carrier-pigeon with a secret
signal from the High Command?

The others clustered round, caught in the mystery of the
moment, holding their breath while I unfolded the curled
slip. It made a dry, rustling sound that could have been heard
twenty yards away. Slowly I opened it out until the pencilled
message lay revealed. It was in English and said simply:
"Bugger you, leave me alone."

There was a moment of shocked incredulity, and then we
burst into simultaneous roars. It was a good ten minutes before we recovered enough wind to start pushing again.

We discussed possibilities. The popular theory, to which I subscribed, was that it had come from our own technical sergeant. It was exactly the sort of thing he would do, and his LAD lorry, a great cavern of a thing filled with all the paraphernalia necessary for keeping a regiment of tanks on the move, became a sort of general depository for everything. Personally, I would not have been surprised if, somewhere in the deep recesses of that ten-tonner, he had a chaise-longue and a couple of Gippo bints. A pigeon was really pretty insignificant stuff for the LAD lorry. The Tech. Sergeant denied all knowledge of the bird when I took it along to him, but I left it there. It seemed to settle in surprisingly quickly.

November 13 was the day on which we heard all about it— the full gen, as it was called. The C.O. had been along to Brigade in the morning and told us in the afternoon. After we had crayoned all the rings and lines and arrows on our maps we went back to our troops to pass on the information, in a state of great exhilaration and confidence. Briefly I told my crews the plan. All three armoured brigades were to be passed through The Wire with our support troops, and backed up by the New Zealand and South African infantry divisions. Most of the German and Italian forces were up in the coastal area, and we were to plonk ourselves down on their lines of communication between them and Benghazi. We were to take up battle positions of our own choosing and destroy the enemy armour when it attacked us. It seemed that the rôle of 4th Armoured Brigade was to do most of the destroying in the centre, while the other two covered our flanks and joined in whenever possible. It seemed a pretty good idea to me, and when I showed the troops my map and where we were going, deep into enemy territory, their eyes popped and their lips whistled. It was all they could do to stop themselves cheering. We were all a bit like schoolboys on the last night of term.

On November 15 we moved forward to the final jumping-off place and, still looking like a field-park of 3-ton lorries, made our final preparations for battle. These preparations included a farewell cocktail party given by the Scots Guards. Two evenings later, at ten minutes to six, with only the shreds of daylight hanging in the western sky, we formed up into long columns of tanks and guns and vehicles and headed west into the night and destiny.

It was soon so dark that the drivers could only dimly discern the outlines of the tank or lorry a foot or two in front of them. It became necessary for the navigator at the head of the column to dismount and walk ahead. So we proceeded slowly through the night, nose to tail, the desert filled with the low-geared roaring of the radials and the creaking protestations of hundreds of springs and bogie wheels. To north and south of us the silence of the empty sands was shattered by similar long, deadly snakes, weaving forward for the strike.

It was not long after midnight when we halted, and the message came back by word-of-mouth (there was an unbreakable wireless silence imposed) that the head of the column had reached The Wire, and there would be no further movement until ordered. I told my crews to get some sleep. "God knows," I said, just to keep them cheerful, "when you'll get another opportunity—unless it's forever." I curled up myself in between the camouflage netting and bed-rolls on the warm bonnet of the engine.

But there was to be little sleep that night. Dimly ahead we could hear the detonations of the explosives as the demolition parties blew the gaps in The Wire through which the Eighth Army were to pass. But soon these puny explosions were mingled with and overwhelmed by a terrific thunderstorm which broke over the coastal area to the north. Vivid flashes of lightning poured swift floods of light over the desert in which the tanks were revealed in grotesque, unreal silhouettes that vanished before the eye could properly comprehend them.

Thunder burst over the escarpments, and rolled across the flat landscape in tidal waves of sound. Men muttered and moved uneasily beneath this bombardment, and made their preparations for the downpour. In our tanks we were lucky under the "sunshields" which we fortified with groundsheets and bivvy tents to make an enclosure which, if not exactly comfortable, was dry. I consoled myself through the storm with the thought that at least it would lay the dust for the morrow.

First Day

THE first grey light in the east awoke me and brought slow, reluctant movement to the whole column. We got permission for a quick brew—the mug of tea which was to become very nearly the most important institution in the desert war. God knows how many gallons of precious petrol were used up during that and subsequent campaigns in bringing kettles to the boil. Half-hearted attempts were made to prevent it while armoured regiments lay stranded with empty petrol tanks, but generals and brigadiers as well as troopers and privates came to recognise the moral effect of "a brew", and it was never seriously discouraged. In the grim days and nights that followed November 18 it was an incredible but not unusual sight to see some tank crew, temporarily immobile or disengaged but still under fire, huddled over a sand-and-petrol stove making tea. It was also inevitable, during any sort of lull in the battle to hear some voice on the air calling up the C.O. and saying "Hullo JAGO, JAGO Two calling. May we brew up?" Once, in the middle of an action down near El Gubi, many days and many lives later, we heard a distinctive Teuton voice saying on our regimental wireless frequency "Hullo BALO, BALO calling. You may brrrew up." The battle paused while the whole regiment rocked with laughter. I have no doubt some died laughing.

Shortly after 7 o'clock we got the order to move. It was a long, jerky and peaceful operation, not at all like the beginning of the great adventure we thought it should be. Petrol dumps had been established during the night a few miles west of The Wire, at which each Honey filled up as it passed. It

was 10 o'clock before my troop reached the gap and passed
through under the control of a number of staff officers and
military police. It was like a passage along Piccadilly in the
rush hour, and a good deal less dangerous for pedestrians.

The excitement returned as we headed at a good pace
north-west into enemy territory towards a point known as
Gabr el Salegh. This, it was expected, would be where we
would fight and defeat the Afrika Korps. The Wire had been
a disappointing thing in its rusty inadequacy, and I think we
all felt a little let-down that, at such a critical moment,
nothing at all had happened. And the sand and scrub of
Cyrenaica looked just the same as the sand and scrub of
Egypt.

We were in the battalion open-order formation now, the
whole brigade moving swiftly towards its first objective. The
hessian disguise still concealed our tanks, but not an enemy
plane appeared all day to give the no doubt surprising information that hundreds of 3-ton lorries were advancing towards Tobruk from the south-east.

At 3.30 in the afternoon the first operational order flashed
through the wireless . . . "Drop Sunshields". The camouflage
fell apart as we rolled on, littering the desert for miles around
and bringing great joy to any wandering Bedouin who could
get to them before the R.A.S.C. picked them up. We quite
often passed isolated groups of Arabs and camels. It was
always a chimerical vision, a glimpse of a world which had
no part in ours.

With the disappearance of the sunshields the wireless
aerials were released, and floating from the top of them were
the twin yellow pennants which each British tank carried for
identification. In moments of quick decision it was assumed
that tanks or armoured cars without pennants were hostile.
Very often the masts were lowered to assist concealment, and

undoubtedly a number of Eighth Army v. Eighth Army encounters took place as a result.

The speed at which we were going, the vast, clean space all round new-washed by the night's rain, and the awareness of participation in great events that possessed us all, restored our feeling of elation. Beyond this excitement I would say that the dominating emotion in my mind was an immense curiosity. Not just about the substantial things of war—tanks and guns and infantrymen and armour-piercing shells. There was an extraordinary inquisitiveness that always possessed me in strange new places and circumstances; but above all there was this curiosity about the immediate future and what would happen in it . . . what would happen to me. Not for one moment did I contemplate the possibility of anything unpleasant, and with that went an assumption that there was bound to be a violent encounter with the enemy, that it would end in our favour, and that if anything terrible were going to happen it would probably happen to other people but not to me.

As we rushed on I was conscious all the time of the vast forces deployed to east and west, and of the screens of armoured cars—South Africans, 11th Hussars, King's Dragoon Guards—which were spread across the desert ahead. We knew that we could hit nothing and nothing could hit us without the air being full of the crackling messages from the recce men in front.

Morning turned to afternoon and afternoon moved on to evening, and the desert stayed empty around us and the skies were as empty as the sands. We lined up again in queues to fill up with petrol. Our radial engines had a very limited range, and we were not to be long in discovering what this could mean in the swift-moving campaign that stretched down the days and nights to come.

At 4.30 we reached our apportioned battle position. A

vaguely discernible cairn of stones marked Point 185 on the trig. survey. A little way to the north lay the equally indeterminate map-name of Gabr Taieb el Esem. We had travelled 65 miles since the dawn. There had been no sign of a German or an Italian. We spent the night more or less as we halted, knowing nothing, but tired enough for sleep to overcome anxiety and puzzlement.

Second Day

BEFORE dawn the next morning we were up and in our action stations, checking the wireless net and listening to the cautious chatter of 'B' Squadron, who were being sent off on a special mission in support of the KDGs. As the light grew we moved off several miles due north, where we sat and watched nothing for another two hours with leisure enough to cook breakfast—bacon, biscuit, marmalade and hot tea.

Then came the message that we had all been wating to hear, flickering through the hundreds of ear-phones on the battalion net: "Hullo DOMO, DOMO calling. DOMO will advance to Bir Gibni to intercept enemy column moving south."

A little surprised at the direction of the move, which was due east of us, we swung round on to the new bearing and moved briskly forward; not as carelessly as the previous day, but eager to start something. One could sense the mounting excitement that spread through each tank and from tank to tank through the whole battalion. In half an hour we reached Bir Gibni, eyes straining from the tops of turrets to the northern and eastern horizons for a glimpse of the significant silhouettes that would mean so much to each of us, one way or another. But the desert stayed flat, and was beginning to look vacuous. Later we were to get used to the daily "swans" into nothingness after nothingness, pursuing mirages of enemy conjured up by imagination and fear, mixed-up communications, mistranslated codes and nerve-wracked commanders.

Later in the day we heard 'B' Squadron reporting that they were trying to engage 7 tanks and 3 armoured cars. We all envied them. In another ten minutes there came the startling order to the remaining two squadrons to advance and engage 200 M.E.T. on the Trigh Capuzzo. I never did find out what M.E.T. stood for—mechanised enemy troops, perhaps?—but we all knew what it implied. 200 M.E.T. meant a long column of German vehicles ready to fall into our armoured lap. Later we were to discover that it also meant tanks and anti-tank guns and the dreaded 88s—the fantastic anti-aircraft guns that the Afrika Korps converted into the war's deadliest anti-tank weapon. Many men were to die on each side of me in finding out exactly what M.E.T. meant.

The Trigh Capuzzo lay well north of the barren well of Gibni. It was an incredible highway stretching from horizon to horizon in an almost dead-straight line, and pounded down to a width of 50 or 60 yards by succeeding convoys all seeking the firm surface alongside the mutilated sand of the preceding column.

There was another brief order, telling 'C' Squadron to attack the head of the column. I brought my troop over a long, low rise which ran down to the Trigh about a mile in front of me. There I paused to let as many tanks as possible of the squadron come abreast of me in a hull-down position while I swept the column with my binoculars. It looked a piece of cake, with only a few armoured cars moving up and down the length of vehicles like shepherd dogs running beside a flock. I saw my other three tanks ready and waiting, and there was Harry alongside me grinning. I gave him the thumbs-up, and with a wide wave of my arm we were off.

We came over that crest 16 abreast and roared down the slope flat out, the wind catching the trailers of dust behind and flaunting them like banners of doom to the eyes of the watchers on the Trigh. We were all caught up in the exhilaration of that first charge. In a few seconds I could see the consternation in the enemy ranks translating itself into violent motion. There was the initial moment of immobility and shock, and then the whole line of vehicles broke and scattered wildly to the north and north-east. Every now and again a vehicle would pull up while its occupants disgorged on to the sand and ran or fell flat.

The main body of the enemy was making good its getaway, and, indeed, had virtually disappeared over one of the numerous escarpments by which the pleateau dropped down to the sea. Maegraith and I were compelled to divert our attention from the fleeing transport to several armoured cars which were beginning to act in a hostile fashion. A couple of small Mark IIs were also bustling about like terriers with their teeth showing. We got two armoured cars and one of the light tanks, and a little later I came across a third one, hurriedly abandoned by the look of it, with petrol still pouring out underneath the engine into a pool on the sand. My gunner put a burst of tracer into the pool, and the whole thing roared up in orange flame and black smoke.

By this time we had left the Trigh Capuzzo miles behind. Some way to my front the land seemed to dip away into space. I guided the driver to the edge of a steepish escarpment, and gasped with astonishment at what I saw. Beyond the intervening belt of rock and sand and scrub rolled the sudden deep blue of the Mediterranean.

"Hells bells, Harry," I yelled into the mike, "I can see the sea."

Over to my right I got another shock. On the end of a promontory stretching out from the escarpment was a squat white building with what I thought was a minaret at one end. Through the binoculars it was revealed as a lighthouse, and beyond that I could just see the roofs and walls of a sizeable village climbing out of a deep wadi below the lighthouse.

"Where the devil am I?" I muttered. Then it came to me. I was looking down on Bardia. I could hardly believe it, but it could be no other place. I scanned the intervening crests and depressions for some sign of the enemy and that column we had been chasing. Then Harry's voice came urgently: "Look out, Bob. There are some anti-tank guns on your left."

Even as he spoke I heard a sharp bang, and felt a slight shudder pass through the tank. I looked quickly down into the turret. There was nothing wrong in there, and I gave the order: "Driver reverse . . . advance left-about . . . speed up."

600 or 700 yards away, along the edge of the escarpment, little men moved agitatedly about a toy cannon. There was a puff of whitish smoke, and immediately I was conscious of something passing by in the air. It was time to get away.

The other tanks were clustered behind a couple of camelthorn bushes, and I thought how funny it was to duck instinctively behind something which could not possibly give any protection. I joined them behind the bushes and shouted at them that we'd better be getting back.

For the first time that afternoon I was able to take stock of time and place, and I was a little worried to see how low the meagre sun had sunk, turning the overcast a stormy red. A few lonely, derelict lorries and armoured cars littered the plateau, and several billowing uprights of smoke signalled the news of our first kills. I counted all seven tanks of our two troops, but of the rest of the squadron and the battalion there was no sign. Through the mike I spoke to Maegraith running alongside:

"Where the devil is everybody, Harry? Has the C.O. been on the air?"

"I haven't seen anybody else since we crossed the Trigh. We've been trying to raise the C.O. for the last twenty minutes, but can't get an acknowledgment."

I was not particularly concerned at that stage. There was no sign of any enemy on all that wide plain or along the clean-cut ridges. All I had to do was keep the sunset on my right shoulder, and I was pretty sure of getting back to friendly territory. The one thing that disturbed me was the petrol situation. We had come a long way since morning, and I did not fancy being stranded so far from base.

As the light failed I picked out a small group of armoured cars to the south, and we altered course slightly to approach them. I reckoned if they were enemy we could cope with them, while if they were friendly they would soon recognise the Honeys, which were like nothing else in the desert.

As we drew nearer I noticed a couple of men walk casually away from the cars towards us, and realised with considerable relief that the troop must belong to our own recce screen. I pulled up alongside and jumped down.

"Hullo," a young KDG subaltern said. "You had us worried for a bit, but there's no mistaking that shape. Where the dickens have you been?"

I told him briefly of our adventures, and then asked him for directions back to 3R.T.R. All he could tell me was a rough map reference for Brigade H.Q., and I decided to head that way and try and get in touch by wireless as we got nearer. Our course was south-west now, with barely ten minutes of light left in the sky and visibility at ground level reduced to a meagre hundred yards. Then I felt the tank moving jerkily, and got a tug on my trousers.

"Whaley says we're out of petrol," my gunner shouted up at me.

I swore quickly, and then got on the air to the other tanks and told them to halt. The tank commanders came over. We had a quick conference, and decided that as all tanks would shortly be out of petrol we would leaguer where we were and try and get into communication with H.Q. The blackness of night was upon us now, and we felt fairly secure in its im-penetrability. I formed the tanks into a solid ring with guns facing outwards. My operator started yelling, and while I was still telling him not to make such a bloody row he shouted that he had got the C.O. on the air.

I jumped on to the turret, and swiftly explained the posi-tion. The C.O. said briefly that he had been trying to get us back all the afternoon and asked for our position. I made a very wild estimate, and he said he would send a petrol lorry out to me. There would be an officer with a wireless set, and we would have to guide him as much as possible. I handed the mike back to the operator, and told him not to let go of that petrol lorry—or else we'd all be in the bag, or worse, in the morning. Then I prayed that I had not been too far out in my map reference, which placed us about five miles from the battalion leaguer.

Half an hour later the replenishment officer came on the air to tell us he was on his way, and would we let him have some toffee apples. This was the irrelevant name used for tracer bullets fired skyward in the night to indicate position. As long as it did not coincide with an air raid, it was an ade-quate signal, and had the great merit of brevity, lasting just long enough for the expectant watcher to take a bearing. I got Maegraith to stand by with a tommy-gun, and then said into the mike: "Toffee apples coming up . . . now!" Harry pulled the trigger for about two seconds, filling the silence with an alarmingly staccato racket while the red dots streamed upward into the darkness. I had the phones glued to my ears and for a few moments there was an awful silence. Then the blessed words: "Have seen your toffee apples. Com-ing in soon. Watch out for me."

It was well after midnight when we slunk into the battalion leaguer. The C.O. was still a bit peeved about our disappear-ance, but was mollified when I told him of our quite successful little raid. To our astonishment the other half of 'C' Squadron was still missing, and did not, in fact, get back until after sunrise.

The Colonel put us in the picture. There had been a heavy attack on 8th Hussars in the afternoon, and it was to go to their assistance that all our tanks had been so urgently needed. Other officers told me how they had seen the Hussars charging into the Jerry tanks, sitting on top of their turrets more or less with their whips out. "It looked like the run-up to the first fence at a point-to-point," the adjutant described it.

This first action was very typical of a number of those early encounters involving cavalry regiments. They had incredible enthusiasm and dash, and sheer exciting courage which was only curbed by the rapidly decreasing stock of dashing officers and tanks.

Very early on in that campaign I learnt when to be gallant and when to be discreet, and how to employ both characteristics to the best advantage of myself. Nearly every risk had to be calculated; bravery, as far as I was concerned, became a matter of judicious discrimination and making the most of an opportunity. It is, after all, of very little use to yourself or your army to be very brave and very dead.

That night, back in leaguer and shared security, I was full of confidence. We had put the enemy to flight, done him some damage and were unharmed ourselves. Maegraith and I returned to our troops from the C.O. feeling rather pleased with ourselves and looking forward to daylight and its possibilities.

When I got back, the LAD gang were at work under the Honey, with all the paraphernalia of repair littering the sand in the concealed island of light.

"What's wrong, Sergeant?" I asked.

"You mean you don't know, sir? Christ, you've had a whole bogie wheel shot off. Any other sort of tank you wouldn't have gone ten yards."

I remembered the crack and shudder on the escarpment, saw again the puff of smoke and felt that invisible thing rushing past me through the air. I gave the side of the Honey a little pat and settled down into the blankets to get as much sleep as the clanging mechanics would allow me. They worked hard right through the night, but the job could not be done in time, and before first light we had to change equipment, food, bedding and crew with another tank. It was something I was to get pretty used to.

That evening a war correspondent called Randolph Churchill, gleaning colourful items for his readers, sent a message back to Cairo that "Bob Crisp, the South African fast bowler, had got the first hat-trick of the Crusader campaign by knocking out three enemy tanks with three shots."

It was duly pinned up on the notice board at the Gezira Club. It was only a slight exaggeration.

In another part of the desert that night, men of the German Reconnaissance Unit 3 were recording in their diary an attack by the enemy: "He had very fast tanks, and the Unit had to get away at full speed under continuous fire. The enemy forced the Unit farther north over the Trigh Capuzzo and the first escarpment and then withdrew south-east."

Nobody else believed my story that I had looked down into Bardia that afternoon.

Third Day

Up to now everything had gone more or less according to plan, and the British armour was where it was intended to be. There was only one thing wrong. The Germans had not reacted; we just had not had that big slogging match that was supposed to happen with the panzer divisions. And sneaking through the battalions on our side were disturbing stories that the Honeys and Crusaders were no match at all for the Mark IIIs and Mark IVs in equal combat. It was a simple proposition: our little cannons could not knock them out, and they could knock us out easily. The word "eighty-eight" was invading the tank-crew vocabulary as a symbol of shattering mutilation. Within the week we were reckoning that it needed three Honeys to destroy one Mark IV, and during that entire campaign we were to find no effective answer to the enemy's use of anti-tank weapons well forward with his panzers. It was a technique that very nearly won him the battle—and many subsequent desert battles in the years to come.

Nobody had time even to make a brew in the morning; as soon as it got light enough to see, shells started falling among us from goodness knows where. Unseen shellfire can be very disconcerting and there is none of the psychological relief of retaliation. We had no sooner got dispersed when tanks were reported, attacking the battalion's right flank. We took up hull down positions to meet this threat, but within half an hour they were reported attacking our left flank. This threat proved equally nebulous, and for 2 hours we sat gazing into space and sand. Away in the distance I spotted a column of vehicles replenishing with petrol, but could not be sure which side they belonged to. Neither could anybody else.

The next alarum came over the air at noon, in the form of a warning to expect a heavy attack from the north where tanks and transport were massing. We were reassured by the information that the Royal Air Force was about to bomb this concentration. There had been plenty of air activity all morning; the first we had seen. The bombers never appeared where we could see them, but the message was good for morale.

By this time most of us were developing a sort of wolf-wolf complex, but we were startled into reality by a frantic call for help from 'B' Squadron, who screamed that they were being attacked by over 100 tanks. The desert air was suddenly full of high explosive and the terrifying swish of armour-piercing shells. Coming in from the west very fast, with the sun behind them shining straight into our gunners' eyes, were scores of the dark, ominous shapes of German panzers. Going even faster a few hundred yards ahead of them were 'B' Squadron's Honeys, together with half a dozen soft-skinned vehicles.

They came hurtling back through 'A' Squadron, whose commander started yelling into his microphone: "Halt! Halt! the lot of you. Turn round and fight, you yellow bastards. I'll shoot the next tank I see moving back."

As that rush came abreast of me and the firing began to get personal, it was desperately hard not to turn round and join in it. I decided not to. At the same time I didn't particularly want to die at that moment. Movement was the obvious answer, but movement in a direction which could not be described as running away. I could see the panzers clearly now, coming down a broad depression in line abreast, 40 to 60 of them, easy enough to exaggerate into a hundred and more. On my left was a low ridge, the southern edge of the depression, and I made for this flat out with my troop conforming, in the hope of getting on the flank of the advancing juggernauts and getting out of the direct line of fire.

Once over the ridge I turned back along the crest to see what was happening, and whether it would be possible to do any damage. The enemy onslaught was losing some of its impetus, owing to lack of opposition, and with darkness falling fast the Germans could not have claimed a great deal of success—although it must have given them a good deal of self-satisfaction. I noticed that two other Honeys had joined my troop, and I led them in a wary circle to try and come up behind some of the flank Mark IVs.

Dimly in the dusk I saw the outlines of a couple of armoured cars, perched on the edge of the depression with both guns firing away to the east. I could not tell in that light whether they were British or German. It was a pity to miss such a nice opportunity to bag a couple of Jerry 6-wheelers, if they were Jerry, so I decided to make a quick dash up to them to get a positive identification. If they turned out to be enemy I could quickly let my other tanks know, and they could knock them out.

I made a hand-signal to the troop sergeant to wait where he was, and ordered my driver to speed up. No concealment was possible now, but I hoped to get up close enough before being seen. I got to within 30 yards of those two cars before I could be sure of the black cross painted on the turret. Then I told the driver "Left about", and swung round in a great plume of sand and dust while I picked up the mike to tell my troop to open fire.

Too late I saw that my hand signal had been either unseen or misinterpreted. 5 Honeys were pursuing me hell-bent in the gloom, one of them hurtling straight down on me. I could not warn my driver in time, but managed to divert him enough to avoid a broadside-on collision. There was a rending crash, and I found myself inextricably locked with the driving sprocket and tracks of the oncoming Honey. Out of the turret popped the ferocious face of the 'A' Squadron commander.

The two armoured cars, clearly disturbed by this unusual display just behind them, disappeared rapidly into the night. We disentangled ourselves but my driving sprocket was hopelessly bent and my Honey had to get towed into leaguer. It was a considerably depleted and dispirited battalion that herded together that evening. What we wanted most of all was information. What the hell was happening everywhere? Was this just the outside edge of a major battle? Who was winning?

There were no replies.

One of the operators got the B.B.C. 9 o'clock news, and we gathered round to hear the familiar, well-modulated voice saying: "The Eighth Army with about 75,000 men excellently armed and equipped, has started a general offensive in the Western Desert with the aim of destroying the German-Italian forces in Africa."

We were not the only troops listening to the 9 o'clock news that night. The German monitors heard it, too. It was the vital piece of information that Rommel was lacking. The advance of Eighth Army into Libya had been so well concealed from the enemy that until they heard the B.B.C. announcement they were wholly unaware that this was a major offensive. Indeed, until the last moment Rommel persisted in his view that the British were not capable of mounting a full-scale attack at that time.

That B.B.C. announcer really started something. Rommel, unaware that anything more than a reconnaissance-in-force had been projected, did not react in the way anticipated by our planners, and during the two days in which he had been expected to give battle to our concentrated forces he had simply sat comparatively quiet trying to get information.

In these two days the Eighth Army Commander, anxious to provoke some sort of decisive action and disturbed at his own inability to exert any influence on the situation, sent his three armoured brigades probing offensively across Rommel's supply lines and towards the rear of the enemy forces investing Tobruk. It broke up the armoured concentration at a decisive time, and split it into three separate parts, each part inferior to the opposing tank force and unable to give quick assistance to each other.

Operation Crusader and the war in the Middle East was very nearly lost simply by Rommel's unbelief and inaction in those first two days. Now things were to start happening. The nights were no longer dark and silent. Our own leaguers remained tombs of rest and replenishment but the Germans, seeking protection in visibility, adopted exactly the opposite night-time tactics and lit the desert all round their leaguers with brilliant white and green flares and Very lights fired continuously by their outlying pickets. It was a convenient arrangement, and it was just as well that at least one side knew where the other was during the hours of darkness.

That night I got orders to take my troop out before first light to patrol the area ahead of the battalion, which was to move due north at dawn.

Fourth Day

IN the cold dark of the pre-dawn my troop moved out of leaguer, hungry, sleepy, dirty, unenthusiastic. I munched miserably at a hard biscuit plastered with marmalade passed up to me from inside the turret where the crew were having their breakfast. The tanks edged forward slowly. In each vehicle the scene would be the same . . . the driver, hands at the ready on the steering sticks and foot poised sensitively on the throttle, would be peering intently at the narrow world confined by the slit in the armour-plating in front of him; the operator would be fiddling about with the wireless set and checking the ammunition and the A.P. shells for the 37-mm.; the gunner would be settling himself comfortably, testing the traverse and the ammunition belts, squinting through his telescopic sights at the rounded O of desert beyond; each tank commander, standing upright in the turret or perched on top with legs dangling inside, would be pushing his vision to the utmost distance to pick up shape or movement, the constant earphones in position and the mike on his chest to maintain his link with the rest of the regiment and with his crew below.

The light stole softly across the desert from the east, and as it drifted ahead it suddenly lit up a dense column of transport moving at a good pace across our front to the north-west. We must have spotted each other simultaneously, as the head of the column suddenly wheeled sharply to the west and made off fast enough to prevent us getting any guns into action.

A brisk battle developed over on the extreme right, and in mid-morning 'C' squadron was moved across to reinforce the other squadrons which were under pressure. On the way past H.Q. I had a quick word with Doctor Macmillan, our M.O., who told me that Peter Williams had been killed. Peter had been second in command of 'B' Squadron, and had got an M.C. at Calais in the evacuation of France. He was the first officer fatality in 3R.T.R., and somehow his death subtly altered the outlook for everybody. A few minutes later I passed Williams' tank where it had been knocked out, and realised with a shock that although it was facing north towards the enemy, the shell which had knocked out the tank and which had killed him had penetrated the back of the turret.

I wondered how many people in the war had been and would be killed by their own sides' bullets, shells and bombs. Identification in the confused, swift-moving desert war was always difficult, and was made more so by encounters that took place so often in the indeterminate light of dawn or dusk and by the paucity of information available about the movements of either force.

It was a confused day of constant skirmishing with enemy forces which seemed to occupy all the desert to the north. I had several duels with enemy tanks, knocked out two and learnt a great deal. I learnt which of their armoured fighting vehicles I could take on and beat with the Honey, and which of them I had to avoid until I could create a favourable situation for myself. We were always prepared to take on any number of Italian tanks, for instance, and any of the German Mark IIs and armoured cars. The Marks III and IV, however, had to be dealt with by subterfuge and the grace of God rather than by superior fighting qualities.

It was on this occasion that I actually saw two A.P. shells coming towards me before they hit my tank. I had picked out a couple of Mark II tanks that had swanned out from the main convoy, as was their habit under threat of attack, and I was making my way towards them using the ground as well as I

could to get within the 600 yards that I had already decided
was the absolute maximum effective range of the 37-mm.
They could see me, of course, and knew what I was up to.
Suddenly I saw the puff of smoke from one of them, and in
the same split second I glimpsed a black object whishing
through the air at me. It was followed immediately by another
shot from the second tank, and exactly the same thing happened. I watched both shells pitch into the sand about ten
yards in front of the tank and ricochet on to the armour with
a devil of a clang. It was an invaluable lesson to me. I had
noticed the quick curvature of the shells, and knew that at
that distance, not above 1,000 yards, the Mark IIs could do me
no damage. More important, I knew that in those German
tanks were some very windy soldiers—much more windy
than I was.

That day, I believe, we shed our light-heartedness and
eagerness. The sense of adventure had gone out of our lives,
to be replaced by grimness and fear and a perpetual, mounting weariness of body and spirit.

In the evening we were ordered to take up positions for an
attack in force on another big enemy column that could be
seen moving to the north-west. Tired and a little unwilling,
we waited for the command that would set us off. The light
failed before it came. Instead, we pulled back into leaguer in
the darkness and counted the rising toll of battle.

The events of that day and the change in the course of the
whole campaign had been determined the previous night by
Rommel, who had issued orders to his two panzer divisions—
15th and 21st—to get together and "attack and destroy the
enemy force which has advanced on Tobruk".

"The objective," added Rommel's order, "is the centre airfield at Sidi Rezegh."

Fifth Day

IN the middle of the night the troop leaders were dragged out of their sleep to go to the C.O.'s tank, where, under a carefully shaded torch, we were shown the plans for an attack with the Royal Horse Artillery battery on an enemy leaguer at dawn. We went back to our hard beds muttering and grumbling. I had always favoured a full-scale night attack on a German leaguer, for the simple reason that I couldn't think of anything worse happening to us, but I didn't particularly want to get mixed up in this one. I was too damn sleepy, for a start.

At four o'clock we were up and moving into the night, and within half an hour all the lightly-armoured towing vehicles of the R.H.A., known as quads, had got bogged down in a swamp which had survived from the last heavy rains. By the time we reached the scene of the intended assault all that was left of the enemy leaguer were the track marks in the sand.

To compensate for this disappointment, we carried out a vicious little assault on a cluster of enemy vehicles, all of which proved to be derelict. This was a not altogether unusual occurence. Movement from leaguer started, of necessity, with visibility at a minimum, and practically anything could happen in that first hour before the sun lit up the desert. The same sort of thing happened in the last hour of light. In between these dim-lit hours the nature of the terrain and atmosphere gave rise to all kinds of queer distortions, so that bushes looked like tanks and tanks looked like rows of trees; and a herd of camels, grazing peacefully in the distance, could fill the air with urgent signals about enemy tank concentrations

—signals which could go from troop to regiment to brigade, the resulting flap penetrating right back to Army Head-quarters. My own tank must have covered many scores of miles literally in pursuit of mirages.

It was an inauspicious start to the day, and it maintained its character throughout the morning, when we set off on three separate "swans" which turned out to be wild-goose chases. Time was so full of purposeless movement that we were unable even to make a brew.

At 1.30 in the afternoon an order was given for the whole regiment to move on a bearing of 283 degrees, 'C' squadron leading. That meant me, and I was wondering how long it would be before the orders were cancelled and replaced by another bearing, when I heard the C.O. say: "Friends like us are being heavily attacked. They need our help. We must move quickly."

At this stage of the fighting so many tanks had broken down or been knocked out that no squadron was at full strength, and troop organisation was on a very make-shift basis. My own troop consisted of only two Honeys, and I had an officer, Tom Eynon, in the other tank acting as troop ser-geant. I lined my tank up on 283 degrees, and the two of us set off at a good pace into the empty desert westwards.

We were soon miles ahead of the rest of the battalion, and I was beginning to think that this was just another false alarm when ahead of me I saw the tell-tale columns of black smoke, like treacle rising, on the horizon. Behind me as I looked back I could see the moving dots of the other tanks, and be-hind them, I knew, were the two other tank regiments of 4th Armoured Brigade, mustering about 100 all told instead of the full quota of 160.

Through the wireless I got in touch with the C.O., who sounded faint and distant, to try and get information about where exactly we were going and what I could expect to find

when I got there. He could tell me nothing beyond the compass bearing. I decided not to wait for reinforcements to come
up, but to press on as fast as possible and get some real information that would be of value to the commanders behind
me. I looked over at Tom, who had heard the conversation,
and who made a despairing gesture with both hands out of
the top of the turret. I gave my driver the order to advance,
and told the crew to get ready for practically anything. The
compass was no longer necessary with that grim beacon to
guide us.

Operation Crusader was now approaching its dreadful and
fateful climax. That bearing of 283 degrees was not just a line
drawn across the desert floor. It was pointed straight at the
airfield of Sidi Rezegh.

The position, briefly, on that Saturday morning was that
light British forces—infantry, guns and tanks of 7th
Armoured Brigade and Support Group—were in occupation
of the airfield and a good portion of the escarpments which
flanked it north and south. Their objective was to link up with
the sortie from Tobruk which had already started. 22nd
Armoured Brigade were still to the south, and 4th Armoured
were as I have just described them. The German armoured
divisions had started their advance from the south-east, to
carry out Rommel's instructions "to destroy the enemy forces
at Sidi Rezegh."

I altered course slightly north, so that my tank was pointing straight at the tall columns of doom. Towards the west
there were some lonely-looking vehicles perched on the rim
of the horizon, and soon, as we sped on, I could pick out long
lines and clusters of transport scattered all over the desert to
my left. But there was nothing to prepare me for the astonishing sight that greeted me as, quite suddenly, I came on to the
edge of a long escarpment which dipped down under the
very tracks of my tank. 30 yards away on my right I saw

Tom's Honey come to a quick halt, and then his voice came
incredulous over the air: "Jesus Christ, Bob! what the hell
is all this?"

Straight ahead and below, in the middle distance, lay the
square, clean pattern of a desert airfield, its boundaries marked
by neat lines of wrecked German and Italian fighter planes, its
centre littered with limp and shattered tanks from some of
which the smoke was rising black into the blue sky. On my
left the desert stretched away covered with thin-skinned
vehicles, but strangely empty of human movement. On my
right, and between our two tanks and the landing ground, the
slope and bottom of the escarpment was crawling with the
dark figures of men digging slit trenches, putting down mines,
clustered around anti-tank and field guns or, unbelievably,
cooking a meal. On the other side of the depression the opposite escarpment was full of men, less active than those below,
and every now and again I saw the flash of gunfire.

Neither Tom nor I could tell whether any of the men,
vehicles or guns were enemy or friendly. The only positive
identification we had were the tanks on the airfield . . . all
the burning ones were British Crusaders. There was no sign at
all behind me of the rest of the battalion, but I just managed
to raise the C.O., very faint and faraway. I told him roughly
where I was, and described the fantastic scene below me. "I
don't know whether they are enemy or friends," I ended.
"Can you tell me what is supposed to be here?"

He told me to wait while he consulted Brigade. In a minute
or two, back came his surprising reply: "Treat anything you
see as enemy."

I was looking across at Tom as the C.O. spoke, and even at
30 yards I could see the reaction of amazement on his face
as he heard the message. We were perched on the edge of the
escarpment in full view of the massed forces about 600
yards below. I could see them looking at us, but nobody

paid much attention. I had come to the conclusion that they must be our own troops, but I could not be positive, and that last bit of information didn't help much. I was quite certain that the people on the other escarpment were enemy, and I was actually able to watch the gunfire and the burst of the shells in the depression below me. Whatever it was, it was a situation that did not seem possible in a battle.

I was nearly going crazy in trying to identify something and trying to determine where the enemy began and ended, and all the time asking the C.O. for information which he could not give me. I told Tom that I was quite sure that the infantry dug in about 2,000 yards away to the north were Jerry and that I was going to engage them with the machine gun. I had already given the gunner the order: "Browning, traverse right. On, two thousand. Enemy infantry . . ." when I heard somebody shouting and banging on the side of the tank. I looked down at a little open tourer that had pulled up alongside and found myself staring at the three pips and crown of a tall, lean brigadier who was standing up on the front seat. I took the ear phones off to hear him ask: "Are you in command here?"

I looked again at his shoulder just to make sure, and said: "I'm in command of this troop, sir."

"What unit are you with?"

"Third R.T.R., 4th Armoured Brigade."

"Good. There's a Jerry tank attack coming in from the west. We need you. Follow me."

I said desperately: "Sir, if you wait ten minutes the whole brigade will be up."

"If you're there in ten minutes you'll be in time. If you're there in fifteen you'll be too late," said the long brigadier. "Follow me."

He sat down, said something to the fair-haired driver sitting capless beside him, and shot off down the escarpment. I

told my driver to follow the car, and we bounced down. Over
my shoulder I could see Tom's tank lurching down behind.
On the way I explained as well as I could what had happened
to my C.O.—that at that moment I was hurtling towards an
airfield on which there were a lot of knocked-out tanks, and
that if he got there in 10 minutes he'd be in time and if he
got there in 15 minutes he'd be too late. I said that as near
as I could judge I was just east of Point 176 on the map, and
that anything he saw between him and the airfield was
friendly. I could do no more, and was very relieved to hear
the distant acknowledgment.

By this time we were down the slope and in amongst the
infantry and gunners. They were our own all right; the grimy,
weary men looked up hopefully as we passed, and I could see
them yelling and giving big "Thumbs-up" signs. We went
through and beyond them in a cloud of dust. 20, 25, 30
miles an hour until the bounding tank, bucking the ridges
and bushes and trenches, stretched out on the sudden smooth-
ness of the landing ground with its crumpled planes.

30 yards ahead of me raced the little car, the blond head
of the driver gleaming like the plumed helm of Navarre. Beside the driver sat the brigadier holding aloft a blue and white
flag that stood straight out in the gale of their going. No
wonder the dispirited troops cheered. It must have been quite
a sight.

Straight across the airfield we hurtled, towards the dipping
sun. I hadn't the faintest idea where we were going, nor why.
I was following three pips and a crown and a stiff, blue and
white flag. Now we were amongst the still-burning, depress-
ing-looking Crusaders, and left them behind to speed through
a few knocked-out Jerry tanks—a much pleasanter sight.
Then we were through these on to the clean desert floor.

Suddenly the shells rained down and the flat surface was

transformed into fountains of red and yellow earth and flying stones and lead through which the little car weaved and dodged and sometimes disappeared altogether in cascades of evil-smelling dirt and smoke. Miraculously it tore on and the arm that held the lofted flag never wavered.

At last, on the opposite edge of the airfield, where the scrub grew again in a straight line, the car halted and my driver pulled back on the brakes. The long brigadier stood up, looked back at me, then waved his arm widely to the westward. In the same gesture the car revved up, doubled back and like a coursing hare disappeared erratically through the shell bursts.

I looked ahead to where the brigadier had swung his arm. My stomach turned over. 1,200 yards ahead of me, stretched the array of dark brown shapes, 60 or 70 monsters in solid line abreast coming steadily towards the landing ground . . . towards me. The vicious flashes at the end of their gun muzzles stood out in fearful contrast against their sombre camouflage. Behind them the sky was red with blood. I didn't need binoculars to pick out the Mark IIIs and IVs. In between moved the infantrymen, and I caught the crackle of machine-gun fire.

I picked up the mike to speak to the gunner: "Cannon. Twelve hundred. You see all those things coming towards you. They're Jerry tanks. Pick out one and stay on it till you knock it out. Get cracking." I heard the first shot go off almost immediately, and watched the tracer sail in a long shallow curve. It hit on one of those dark silhouettes, and bounced high into the air. We were much too far out of range to do any great damage, but I had to do something, and we were well within their range. I kept my gun going more in hope than expectation. Anyway, it was good for morale. We couldn't just sit there.

My own feeling of nakedness and exposure was complete. There wasn't a bush more than two feet high anywhere to provide even the illusion of concealment. I looked round wildly for any kind of undulation that would give me even an imaginary protection, but the only unevenness on all that level plane was the churned-up sand of earlier tank tracks. In the event it was probably my immobility which saved me.

Over on my right I suddenly saw Tom's Honey coming flat out across the landing ground. He came up almost abreast of me, and was about 100 yards off when suddenly, still at top speed, his tank gave a great swerve and, slewing up sand as a speedboat splashes water, wheeled completely round and vanished somewhere among the derelict tanks.

It was those knocked-out tanks which, I believe, saved me. The German tank gunners could not have been able to distinguish whether they were derelict or in action, and it is very unlikely that they would have expected to be confronted with one, solitary Honey. I looked quickly over my shoulder expecting to see the depression full of the charging, pennanted tanks of the whole 4th Armoured Brigade. My spirits dropped when I realised that on that whole vast airfield not a thing was moving.

The red fountains were playing all round me now; my mouth was filled with the acrid taste of cordite, and my nose could sense that frightful smell of impending death that goes with it. The air was full of lead and noise, and the tanks crept towards me with their guns belching. Mingled with the detonations of the H.E. and my own cannon I could hear that terrifying swish of armour-piercing shell, and sometimes get a split-second glimpse of a tracer going by, taking the breath out of my lungs with the vacuum of its passage. Every now and again my Honey would give that quick lurch which meant a hit.

I heard my gunner yell "I've got one, sir," and it sounded good to hear his elation and to see the slow smoke curling up from the Mark III and the men bale out. The gunner was all right. He was picking his targets with an occasional word from me as I watched the tracer searing towards its target: "Keep on that big bastard that you've just hit until you stop him." The loader was all right, too. He would be too busy to be scared . . . tugging the next shell out of its bracket, pulling down the ejection lever, whipping in a new shell with enough force to close the breech, bending under to tap the gunner in the "gun ready" signal, and then starting all over again as he heard the shot and saw the recoil next to his face. Anyway, he couldn't see what I could see and the gunner could only see a small part of it. The driver was the chap I felt sorry for. He would be squeezed back and to one side, getting as far away from his driving aperture as possible, inactive and frightened to death, staring at that advancing line of tanks with an awful fascination, wondering when the shell would strike that would carve his body into little pieces, sensing the still-running engine through his feet and hands.

I noticed the engine, too, the sweet music of the radial in between all the other sounds and the little rocking movements that were sometimes a strike and sometimes the recoil of my own cannon. I was still on the air to my C.O.: "Hullo JAGO, JAGO one calling. Seventy enemy tanks approaching western edge of airfield. Am engaging at a thousand yards. JAGO one to JAGO, over."

I was blurting my message into the frantic signals which were jamming the regimental frequency, hoping that somebody would hear me. I never got an acknowledgment.

The arbitrary business we make of time crumbles into nothingness or infinity on occasions like that. I have no means of knowing how long we were on the edge of the airfield of Sidi Rezegh . . . 5 minutes, 20 minutes? Whatever it was, there came a time when it was long enough. I had a last despairing search behind me for some sign of rescue and support, and then I decided to go. The line of tanks ahead of me was only about 800 yards away, but I could see the shell-bursts where our own 25-pounders were beginning to go into action. The line seemed to be slowing down a bit as though it did not know quite what to do, and was awaiting some decisive order. It seemed the psychological moment to make my departure. I said as quietly as I could into the mike: "Gunner, cease fire. Driver, advance . . . turn about . . . go like hell."

That "driver-advance" was the critical moment. It was always the same after a slugging match with the enemy; that frantic second of time when you did not know whether the tank would move or not. Even if the engine is still running, the suspension may be blasted into a state of collapse; either of the tracks may be lying on the sand in mangled pieces; any of those sickening lurches might have meant the end of your last hope—mobility.

On the edge of the landing ground I held my breath and felt the tank heave as the gears engaged. Then the engine seemed to rev high with relief, and the tank moved forward. This was another critical period. As soon as the tank moved, I knew that the eyes of every gunner in those panzers would be attracted to me. If the engine stalled now I had had it. In fact, there was a good chance of that whatever happened, but I was quite sure that once I could get up speed I would be able to get away.

We got round the turn-about without disaster, and soon we were speeding back across the airfield, jinking left and right, creating our own smoke-screen of dust, dodging into the smoke of the shell bursts, all of which, as I had anticipated, now seemed to be aimed at me personally. "Driver right, steady. Driver left, steady. Driver right . . . steady." So we fled back running that incredible gauntlet of death, each second beckoning us to safety. When we reached the lee of the derelict tanks we were more or less safe from A.P. shells, and I knew we had made it.

Half-way back across the landing ground I felt safe enough to slow down and consider the situation. There was still a battle to be fought, and I did not want to fight it alone. The rest of the brigade must be somewhere. I halted the tank while I surveyed the scene through my binoculars. Behind me the panzers appeared to have come to an uncertain stop some hundreds of yards from the airfield. The sun was disappearing over the high ground to the west, and there would not be more than half an hour's fighting light left of the day. Feeling more reassured, I turned my attention to the southeast, from where I expected to see the Honeys of 3R.T.R. streaming down the escarpment. All I could see was a vast and swirling cloud of dust, and going round and round inside it in circles and figures-of-eight I could dimly pick out the familiar shapes of British tanks. The battalion frequency was a bedlam of orders and counter-orders and frantic calls for information. For a few precious seconds I managed to get the C.O. on the air, and heard him order everybody else to shut-up "so that I can talk to Bob".

I didn't go into details, but told him that there were about 70 Jerry tanks approaching the airfield from the west. He should get all tanks lined up on the eastern edge of the landing ground facing west. He would find me there. His reply was very much to the point. From somewhere, in the middle of the tank-manufactured dust-storm he said: "I don't know my arse from my elbow, let alone east from west." But I heard him pass the instructions on to the squadrons telling them to line up on my tank.

I saw several tanks come out of the dust, and mill about blindly. Two of them fell into an anti-tank ditch, and through my glasses I could see one lying on its side with the upper track whirling madly. It was a hopeless shambles, and after a depressing few minutes I heard the C.O. order all tanks to rally on top of the escarpment.

I can't say that I wasn't very relieved at this development. The panzers were on the move again, looking even more monstrous in the reflected red of the sky as they surged slowly towards the landing ground and the southern escarpment. Our Honey was coming under direct fire again, so we wasted no time in obeying the latest order.

But something was wrong. The tank was behaving in a very peculiar manner. Then I smelt the smoke. Quickly I looked down into the turret. The white, questioning faces of the gunner and operator stared back at me, and their lips formed the word "Fire". I looked back at the engine and saw the ominous fumes pouring out of the louvres. Just then the Honey stopped. I yelled at the crew to bale out, and as we jumped down on to the sand we grabbed what we could off the hot armour-plating above the engine—bedding, grub, water bottles, cooking utensils. We ran back through the shell-bursts and straggled wearily through the confusion and the gathering night up the side of the escarpment.

The first person I saw was Harry Maegraith. He also was climbing the escarpment with his crew; it was his tank which I had seen toppling sideways into the ditch. I pointed back to the airfield where a fresh, dense column of smoke was rising high above the others.

"There's our Honey," I said, and told him quickly what had happened. "But what the hell happened to everybody?"

"You've never seen such a balls-up. We got to the edge of the escarpment all right, and then nobody knew where to go or what to do. We were told to advance on to the airfield and to line up on you facing west. Then Fifth Tanks got mixed up with us, and between us we kicked up such a hell of a lot of dust that we couldn't see ten yards in any direction. We just went round and round each other in circles. I don't think any of our tanks went into action."

Talking and panting, we reached the top of the escarpment, and soon we picked up a little cluster of Honeys with their yellow pennants fluttering idly in the dirt-filled air. To our relief we recognised our C.O. perched on the turret, earphones on and mike pressed to his lips. When he saw us walking up, he handed over to his operator and jumped down.

"Am I glad to see you," he said. "The whole blasted battalion's disappeared. We've got my own tank and these three others—that's the lot. I've got some of them on the air, but they haven't the faintest idea where they are or where we are. What happened to you two?"

His eyes grew wide with astonishment as he listened to my sketchy story. I was telling him about Tom Eynon, and asking whether Tom had contacted him, when a Honey drew up alongside us and from it clambered the familiar, black-overalled figure of Brigadier Gatehouse. He told us quite calmly that his headquarters had been overrun by a Jerry tank column, and that he wanted some tanks to go with him and get it back. I have never been more grateful to have been knocked out. Nothing could shake Alec Gatehouse out of that rock-like imperturbability. He showed no surprise when he was told that Third Tanks could muster only four Honeys.

"Then I'll go and get some of Dinham Drew's lot," he said, and drove off to 5R.T.R. somewhere east of us along the top of the escarpment. He collected about a dozen Honeys, formed them up in a solid, triangular armoured phalanx and moved off into the desert night. They had a wild Guy Fawkes encounter with an enemy column, but did not get back the brigade H.Q.

The sun was down behind the rugged western escarpment, and the smoke and dust of war were mingling with the darkness, as we strained our eyes into the depression to try and see what was happening. I was quite sure that any minute the squat shapes of panzers would come rumbling through the gloom, but we could see no movement except for the silhouettes of a party of stretcher bearers walking along the rim of the escarpment to the west, steel-helmeted but incredibly unconcerned. Machine-gun bullets were zipping everywhere through the low scrub, and I used the last of the light to study these courageous men through my binoculars. With the exception of the Medical Officer, who was leading them, they were all coloured.

"Good God," I said to myself. "Cape coloureds! That must be the South African brigade over there."

And I saw again that long line of tanks sweeping up from the sunset, and wondered what would happen to the infantry men crouched in their shallow, rocky slit-trenches when the panzers rolled over them. I turned to my C.O.: "Jesus, sir, that brigadier will get a bloody V.C. for today's performance, but I wish to hell he had waited ten minutes."

He got his V.C.; it was Brigadier Jock Campbell.

That night we leaguered where we were, each man sitting in his apportioned place inside the turret. I wondered what the hell had happened to Tom Eynon. I didn't think about tomorrow at all.

Some years later, penned up in England awaiting the invasion of Normandy, I whiled away the time by writing an account of these incredible hours for a Sunday newspaper. My then commanding officer read it in the Mess, asked me if it was true and pointed out that it was very convenient that the only person who could corroborate it, Jock Campbell, was dead. I had come to the conclusion some time before that it was practically impossible for a junior officer to kick a Colonel in the backside and get away with it, especially in an Officers' Mess, so I said nothing.

A few days later a letter arrived for me and, looking quickly at the signature, I was elated to see it was from Tom Eynon. I invited him to come and spend a few days with us and went to meet him at Ipswich Station. He came out of the train on crutches and one leg.

Back in the Mess he told me his story. He had seen the little staff car alongside me, and heard my information going back to the C.O., but couldn't believe his eyes when he saw the car tearing off down the escarpment with my tank just behind it. He got a late start, but was soon pursuing the pair of us towards the airfield several hundred yards behind and going flat out. He saw my Honey stop and then the car came jinking back through the shell-bursts. He was still wondering what it was all about when he spotted the long line of Jerry tanks coming towards the landing ground.

"I was just going to give the driver the order to slow down to pull up in line with you," Tom told me, "when my Honey suddenly swung completely round, still going flat out, and we went back across the airfield lurching crazily from side to side. I thought my driver had gone mad, and was yelling at him through the mike when I felt the operator pulling hard on my leg. He shouted up at me that the driver had been hit."

Just after this the tank had come to a halt of its own accord, and they had all clambered out. Shells had been bursting all over the airfield, and the air had been whistling with bullets. Tom had gone round to the front of the tank to try and get the driver out through the hatch. He had propped open the thick steel flap, and had reached in with both hands to grip the man under the armpits. The driver had been dead or unconscious, and as Tom had leaned back to heave he had felt the gears engage suddenly, so that the Honey lurched forward, bundling Tom over backwards and passing right over him. What had happened, he reckoned, was that the shell had penetrated the front of the tank and killed the driver, whose foot had depressed the clutch pedal and stayed on it until

Tom had tried to pull him out. Then his foot had moved, the clutch pedal had sprung out, engaging the gears, and the tank had started forward.

"When I came out from under that Honey," said Tom, "I didn't know what the hell had happened for a few seconds. I saw the tank disappearing with my crew hanging on to the side and a corpse in the driver's seat. Then I realised my one leg had been more or less snapped off at the hip. That night the Jerries picked me up and sent me to one of their hospitals."

After nearly three years in hospitals and P.O.W. camps, Eynon had been released, under an exchange-of-prisoners scheme, shortly before reading my article. I let him repeat his story to the C.O., without comment.

There was other confirmation, of a sort, at the war's end. Writing of the afternoon's events in the Royal Artillery Commemoration Book, Brigadier Hely described the withdrawal from gun positions on the edge of the airfield: "The advancing German infantry were almost on them. Firing at point blank range, with apparently no hope of survival, these indomitable men still fought their guns. Suddenly a troop of British light tanks roared out of the gathering gloom, charged straight into the German infantry and, firing with every weapon they had, halted the enemy attack long enough for the gunners to hook-in and pull out."

It is surprising how radically a slightly different angle can alter the view! Another example of altered perspective is recorded in the Rifle Brigade's account of the proceedings. After referring to the synthetic dust storm caused by charging tanks and bursting shells, the writer describes how Brigadier Campbell came up to a regiment of the 4th Armoured Brigade, dashed along the line of tanks hammering on their steel sides, explained the urgency of the situation and led them into battle "in a sort of cavalry charge waving a red flag".

I am not the least surprised that on that confused and bloody battlefield the brigadier's blue and white flag seemed red, or that two Honeys could look like a regiment.

One other thing about that Sidi Rezegh evening that always puzzled me has been cleared up subsequently by German war diaries. When I last saw that mass of panzers and infantry, they had nearly reached the edge of the airfield. I could never understand why, during the night or at dawn the next day, the whole depression and the escarpments to north and south of it were not overrun and occupied by the enemy. I knew only too well that there was practically nothing to stop their progress across the landing ground except the empty hulks of tanks and the immobile dead. What had stopped them? The explanation from the German side was a simple one—they had run out of petrol and ammunition.

Thus history is made . . . and written. On the following morning the newspapers of Britain and the Commonwealth had headlined with rejoicing type General Sir Thomas Blamey's comment: "Britain has won the tank battle in Libya".

Many times in the years that have passed I have tried to recapture my personal emotions through the events of that hectic afternoon. At the beginning it is always the same with me. A turmoil in the stomach, which is probably a common experience, giving physical credence to the expression "wind-up". I had had the same feeling many times to a lesser degree waiting for a race to begin or getting ready to bat in a Test match. Then, when the race is begun or the innings started, the fullness of the moment overwhelms the fear of anticipation. It is so in battle. When mind and body are fully occupied, it is surprising how unfrightened you can be. I only remember two moments on the airfield when I felt the shock of fear so strongly that it went to my stomach. There was the first realisation of the long row of panzers coming straight towards me, and there was the sudden awareness, when I looked back over my shoulders expecting to see the Honeys roaring out on to the landing ground, that I was utterly and completely alone.

But they were fleeting emotions, soon secondary to the business in hand and the need not to sound afraid to those other three men below me. I had to stay in command, not only of them, but of time and circumstance. I was bewildered by the whole situation, and, as always, filled with an intense curiosity about what was going to happen next. Running through it all, too, was a sense of elation at what we were doing out there on our own, or trying to do. Also, I was bloody annoyed. Annoyed not with the Germans or Italians, but with brigadiers and generals and colonels and all the blasted armoured brigades and regiments that had left me stranded naked on an airfield within a few hundred yards of a panzer division while they mucked about in an immunity of confusion.

That evening I rolled up in borrowed blankets alongside the adjutant's tank and went to sleep, wondering how the hell we four had managed to be still alive.

Sixth Day

IN Britain, this Sunday, the last in November, is the end of the Ecclesiastical Year. In the German Church calendar it is known as Totensonntag—the Sunday of the Dead—and thus it was labelled for history by the German Afrika Korps. The appelation would have been a good deal more accurate if applied to a kind of All Souls Day of the South African Dutch Reformed Church.

During the night a few stray Honeys had wandered into our little resting place, and at 5.30 on Sunday morning the total available strength of the 3rd Royal Tank Regiment—all 7 of it—was ordered to move south-west on a bearing of 210 degrees. Where the order came from only the colonel knew, as the desert around us was empty of Honeys. There was no sign of Brigade H.Q., nor of 5R.T.R., nor of 8th Hussars, nor of our own 'A' and 'B' squadrons. There was just our battalion headquarters and the remains of two troops of 'C' squadron. We knew where some of our tanks were, all right; they were at the bottom of those columns of smoke which still rose black and thick from the depression, invisible over the escarpment a mile to the north-west. Smoke and dust of yesterday's battle still hung in the unmoving air, and unbelievable whistling came from a random truck some 40 yards away whose crew were making breakfast. As we watched, wondering about the day that was now opening about us, the first red rays caught the columnar crests of smoke, dissipating them in wisps of blood. I thought, for no particular reason, that it must have looked like that when the Israelites were led out of Egypt.

As the tank engines warmed up, the dismounted crews clambered up behind the Honeys until such time as contact could be made with our 'B' echelon lorries and they could go back and await the arrival of new vehicles. I sat on the back of the adjutant's tank—it was warm on top of the engine—wondering how I could get myself a Honey and trying to work out my movements if we ran into a battle. There was little I could do about anything. No transport was available, and there was no place to go to anyway. I was damned if I was going to sit on my arse all day watching the battle of Sidi Rezegh from the edge of the escarpment. I didn't think it was going to last very long, at that.

As the sun lifted red and solid out of the desert, we came into what can only be described as a densely-populated area. Hundreds of vehicles—lorries, trucks, staff-cars, ten-tonners, jeeps, wireless vans, command cars, armoured cars—surrounded us on all sides. Peaceful smoke from dozens of breakfast fires hung lazily over the scene. Looking around me in amazement from my perch on the back of the Honey I was delighted to see the orange shoulder flashes of South Africans, and the friendly but anxious black faces of African troops going about their early morning chores.

We had run into the H.Q. area of the 5th South African Brigade somewhere just south-west of Hareifet en Nbeidat. Our covey of tanks pulled up, and I saw the colonel dismount and start talking to one of the senior officers shaving alongside a staff car. I jumped down, and soon found myself among friends, including Ronnie Grieveson, the Transvaal and South African cricketer, who gave me news of other cricketing contemporaries of mine—Bruce Mitchell was one—scattered around the Western Desert. He also supplied us with inevitable and delicious mugs of coffee, and after one look at me invited me to use his wash basin and shaving kit. A grinning African batman brought a can of hot water; it was just like old times on a shooting trip in the veld. I had managed to get my hands wet and soaped when I heard the adjutant calling my name. He beckoned hurriedly from the turret of his Honey, and I noticed that the C.O.'s tank was already on the move. I managed to splash some of that wonderful hot water on my face, and then ran for it, wiping off the mud with a muddier handkerchief. With much grinning and waving and yelling of rude Afrikaans phrases we went on our way through the vehicles and men and paraphernalia.

Above the roar of the engine the adjutant was bellowing the latest griff. We were to continue on our bearing of 210 degrees until we came to a spot called Hagfet el Garbia. I looked at the map propped on my knees, and saw that this was on the track running from El Adem to the Trigh el Abd, about 5 miles south of our present position. When we got there (the adjutant shouted) we were to link up with our Brigade H.Q., which was somewhere in that area. I wondered how on earth Brigade had managed to get down there, and looked forward to being able to pick up another Honey if there were any left over from the previous night's escapades.

We were crossing a comparatively deserted strip of desert, and I could see the mass of vehicles we had just left slipping down over the horizon behind me. Engrossed in my thoughts and my map-reading I was jerked back to reality by a sudden commotion about the tank. We were engulfed in a mad rush of trucks and lorries scattering over the desert to the north and east, while everywhere soldiers on foot ran for slit-trenches and disappeared incredibly into the sand. I gaped round the corner of the turret, and saw that we had come into another South African leaguer area even vaster and more densely packed with transport of all kinds than the one we had so recently left. Several shell bursts just ahead of us showed part of the reason for the sudden commotion. The adjutant leaned back and yelled into my ear: "You better get off,

Bob. Your South African pals are being attacked by tanks, and we've got to go and help them."

I nodded and jumped off, and ran over to where I could see a few officers trying to get things organised. I noticed a few armoured cars and a couple of Honeys lying around, but who they belonged to I could not even guess. I soon discovered that we were in among the 5th Brigade 'B' Echelon, the entire outfit, and they were in a fine state of flap with enemy tanks apparently all round them. All of a sudden I saw the unmistakeable squat shape of a German Mark III, accompanied by a lesser Mark II, coming right through the leaguer about 100 yards from me. I thought I was seeing things. But they were there all right, turret closed, jinking about a bit, but coming straight for us. Everybody around me suddenly went to ground, very properly. I was unused to this sort of evasive action, and I did what was for me the instinctive thing. I made as fast as I could for the nearest Honey.

It was facing away from the approaching panzers, and as I clambered up the back I could see the commander looking rather abstractedly out towards the west, without a clue as to what was happening just behind him.

"Hey, you!" I yelled, thumping him on the shoulder and noticing with some relief as I did so that he was a sergeant. "There's a Jerry tank just behind you. Shoot it."

He looked up at me blankly, uncomprehending.

"Where are you from?" I shouted. "What battalion?"

"Fourth Armoured Brigade Headquarters," he said, and then, looking at my shoulder, added "Sir."

"Then for Christ's sake, man, get after those tanks."

I pointed to the panzers which were now just going past about 30 yards away, their guns silent, still heading north in a puzzled sort of way, scattering men like a bow-wave from their course.

"This is the signals tank, sir. We've never fired the gun."

"Out," I said. "Quick!"

"But the Brigadier . . ."

I grabbed him by his webbing equipment and jerked him out of the turret. "Never mind the brigadier. I'll fix it when I see him. Out!"

He accepted the situation, bemused and reluctant. I climbed into the turret and grabbed the inter-com mike.

"Driver, advance right. Gunner, get that bloody cannon loaded. You're going to get yourself a German tank in about two minutes."

I don't know what their reaction was. I hoped to hell that the driver knew how to drive and that the gunner knew how to aim and pull the trigger. I didn't even know that there were three men down there. However, the tank started to move, and it went in the ordered direction. The breech block clanged as the shell was rammed in, so that was all right, too. The panzers did not confront me with any serious problem. I had a rough idea of what was happening inside those Jerry turrets. They had gone astray from their column, and were a damn sight more frightened than any of the South Africans they were scattering. We went pretty carefully through the leaguer to avoid running over anybody, and then caught up with the Mark III about 100 yards outside the perimeter. It still seemed in a bit of a daze, wondering where to go. It took my anonymous gunner three shots to hit it, then I saw the tracer going into the engine louvres, and smoke started to roll out immediately. At the same time the turret opened and the crew spilled out. As soon as they saw what was happening the men inside the Mark II got weaving. They shot off into the open space between the two leaguers. I saw a couple of Marmon-Harrington armoured cars closing in on it, and left them to it. The crew of the Mark III started to walk back towards us with their hands raised. I pointed them out to a bunch of South Africans nearby, and they went over to bring them in.

My new crew and I drove happily back through the leaguer.
It felt good to have a tank around me again. Inside the turret
I could see the gunner and operator looking very pleased with
themselves, and I leaned down and patted the gunner on the
back. 'You ain't seen nuthin' yet,' I said to myself, 'poor
buggers.'

The Honey moved carefully through the clustered transport, heading for the southern side where I hoped to find my
C.O. and get under command again. Every now and again a
native would jump up from a slit trench with arms raised in
surrender. I dug into my memory for Zulu and kitchen-kaffir
inanities and cuss-words, and yelled them at those bewildered
blacks. It was great to see the look of incredulity on their faces
and then the sheepishness and the great guffawing and head-
shaking as the situation penetrated. "Ow! This was something else to tell them back at the kraal. The Moff who told me
to 'Hamba lapa kaia kawena' 'when I surrendered. Ow!''

The rest of the battalion Honeys were spread along the
south-facing edge, and we joined them just in time to get
mixed up in a wild and indiscriminate encounter with a
column of German tanks and transport which was moving
north-west across the corner of the leaguer. We all started
blazing away like mad, and with a couple of troops of anti-
tank guns joining in and some 25-pounders thumping away
from somewhere in the rear, the attack—if it was meant to
be an attack on us—was beaten off, and the column moved
off out of range. Two or three enemy armoured cars straggled
about behind the column, and when I thought it discreet
enough, I shot my Honey out towards them to cut them off.
Two of them got away, but I cornered one after a short running fight. We pulled alongside as the white handkerchief
fluttered from the top of the turret, and a very frightened face
looked over the top. I indicated the leaguer, and told him,
with much gesticulation, to get moving. A South African

armoured car came up, and together we shepherded the
enemy vehicle back. When I felt sure he would not try and
get away I left them, and swanned about the now-empty
desert looking for some more easy pickings. It felt nice and
unconfined out there, and I was in no hurry to get back, but
nothing happened, so we moved leisurely towards the leaguer.
The leisureliness was deliberate. That leaguer was rimmed by
a number of trigger-happy gunners, in tanks and behind
2-pounders. Any form of violent movement on their front
could startle one of them into action. After the events of the
past twenty-four hours nobody could be blamed for shooting
first and holding the post mortem later. That was why, as we
drew nearer, I waved my handkerchief over my head and
hoped to God the gunners had studied their tank silhouettes.
Nobody fired, and we moved peacefully into the brigade lines.

I was making for a little cluster of Honeys which had moved
from the southern flank and seemed to be taking up a position
facing west when, without any order from me, the tank came
to a jerky stop. I knew what the answer was before the driver's
message reached me—we had run out of petrol.

I told the crew to dismount, and got down to see if there
was any petrol to be scrounged from the South Africans. At a
nearby lorry a young officer explained that they were very
short themselves, but he would let me have one four-gallon
tin. It was ordinary motor spirit, of course, and I could not
expect to get any high octane stuff from that echelon. I
carried the tin back to the Honey and saw that my new driver
was just climbing out of the front. It was the first time I had
seen him. To my astonishment, he had no sooner got to the
ground than he started running round and round in small
circles with a wild look on his face. The poor chap had just
been in action for the first time in his life, and hadn't the
faintest idea where he was or what he was doing.

The other two members of the crew stood there gaping at

him, but did nothing. I walked quickly over, and as the driver went past on one of his running circles I caught him with a tremendous kick in the backside. It jerked his head back and stopped him in his tracks. I grabbed him by the shoulder, and shook him hard. "Listen. I'm your new tank commander. We're in the South African leaguer. Our Honey has run out of petrol. Here's a four-gallon tin. Now, fill up."

He made a visible effort to pull himself together, rubbed his behind a little, said "Yes, sir," picked up the tin and went to work. I told the wireless operator to get back on the set and try and get on to the battalion net, so that I could keep in contact with my C.O. The gunner came up to say that the machine gun had never been fired, and he'd like to go and check it and the ammo.

"That's the stuff," I told him. "That Browning will be the end of all of us if it doesn't work properly at the right time ... and don't forget to carve yourself a couple of notches on the 37-mm. barrel!"

While the crew were getting things ready I walked over to the edge of the leaguer, and looked out across the desert to the west where, half an hour before, the German column had gone past in a blaze of gunfire, dust and smoke. Where all had been noise and frightfulness the sands were now silent and barren. Suddenly I saw three vehicles come over a low rise and halt on the horizon about two miles away. I could just see men running about in a bustle of activity, and with some curiosity I lifted my binoculars and focused on them. I was flabbergasted to see a troop of German field guns just going into action. As I watched I saw the puffs of smoke from the gun muzzles as they fired round after round in a northerly direction towards the Sidi Rezegh escarpment.

They seemed to be quite oblivious of the presence of enemy troops within two miles of them, though they could not possibly have missed seeing that vast array of transport. They were either completely clueless or completely arrogant. I had already, more or less subconsciously, made up my mind what to do, working out the chances of success, calculating the recklessness required. I searched the desert carefully for any signs of approaching enemy vehicles or for any dug-in infantry and anti-tank guns that might be protecting the battery. There was nothing. The desert was bare. The German gunners were on their own. I ran back to my Honey.

I knew what I was going to do, but I needed a little support, and looked round hopefully, wishing that Harry Maegraith could be alongside me. Down the line of trucks and 2-pounder portees I picked out the familiar turret of one of our tanks. I ran quickly down and climbed up behind the commander, a flamboyant-moustached lieutenant in the 5th Battalion. I didn't waste time asking what the hell he was doing there, but told him quickly about the guns and what I was going to do and that I wanted him to come with me. He looked as though he didn't quite believe what I was saying but then he had a long look through his binoculars, and was plainly impressed by the possibilities, although still reluctant.

"I'd better ask the C.O.," he began rather hesitantly.

"Don't ask him; tell him. Look, you'll see me leaving the leaguer just up there. Follow me."

I jumped down before he had time to argue or think up any of the very good reasons why we shouldn't do it. Back on my Honey everything was set, guns loaded and engine running— even if not too smoothly on that inadequate petrol. The operator hadn't been able to raise the colonel, but that didn't matter for the time being.

"Driver advance," I ordered and steered him carefully through the vehicles before telling him to speed up. We made a wide deviation once we had got clear of the leaguer so that we could come up behind the German guns.

I took one look behind me and saw the other Honey following on. Then gave all my attention to my little plan. We were doing a good 30 miles an hour now, and the success of the whole venture depended upon getting right up to the Germans before they saw us. There was no difficulty about anticipating their immediate reactions. If they didn't run like hell they would swing their guns round and try and knock us out; but as the barrels were pointing up at the sky somewhere to give them the range to the escarpment, it was not a thing to cause a great deal of concern. It was simply a matter of timing. If they saw me in time to swing their guns round and depress them, then we had had it. If we were able to get on top of them unnoticed, there was no danger. Every second made us more secure. The other Honey was swerving round behind me—not going quite as fast as I wanted him to perhaps, but it wasn't his idea anyway. Certainly there was no time for slowing down and waiting for him to catch up. It did not matter much where he was; in fact, the mere sight of him steaming up would be enough to accentuate and maintain the impression I was sure of creating.

Three hundred yards to go, and the German guns were still firing northwards, their gunners engrossed in their occupation. Another second or two and I could see clearly the gun teams going through their well-drilled loading and firing and re-loading movements. Not a single head was turned in my direction. Already I knew I had eliminated the possibility of being blown to bits by any of those shells unless something went very wrong at my end. After a certain point of time and distance, I was in command of the moment. It is a fine feeling.

With about 150 yards to go someone suddenly spotted me. I could almost hear the wild yell of fright and alarm, and see the look of unbelief and consternation as every visible face turned towards the racing tank. Then the Jerries scattered from behind their guns, and I gave a sharp order: "Driver, slow down . . . halt. Browning, men and guns, fire!"

The tank pulled up not 50 yards from the enemy, and as we lurched to a standstill the Browning barked briefly. I watched the sand flick up around and beyond the guns. I waited for the next burst, and then sensed with some dismay that the blasted gun had jammed. At the same time I saw the field-gun nearest me swinging round as a couple of men behind it—a good deal braver than the rest—worked feverishly to get it round and trained on the Honey. I wasn't particularly worried, as I could see the barrel still pointing upwards at an angle of about 45 degrees; but there wasn't going to be all that amount of time, and above all I had to maintain the psychological impact. I gave another order down the intercom: "Thirty-seven, nearest field-gun, fire."

There was a pause of about three seconds as tank and gun crew worked desperately to get the first shot in. The Jerries never had a chance. They had managed to get their weapon swivelled round roughly in my direction and then, panic-stricken, one of them had pulled the trigger. I heard the bang, saw the smoke and heard the whoosh of air above me all in one split second. Every detail of the faces of those three men is etched on my memory. I could see the unshaven growth on cheeks and chins. I could see duty and courage struggling with fear and contorting their faces into awful grimaces. The man nearest me was feverishly turning a handle which was depressing the gun slowly; the muzzle was dropping inch by inch. Just behind him another man had picked up a shell and was slamming it into the breech. Around the corner of the gun I could see half a man crouched in an aiming position. It was three seconds of time encompassing half a dozen lifetimes. It took my gunner three seconds to get the cross-wires trained on the heart of that field-gun. Then he pulled the trigger. The whipcrack of the 37-mm. hit my ears, and I saw the quick, dull-red circle glow in the solid metal of the gun in front of me. The Germans dropped to the sand. Immediately one got up and hobbled off, his right hand holding his leg just above the knee, the other arm raised in a gesture of surrender. The other two men lay where they had fallen, and I did not see them move again. The second Honey pulled up alongside, its guns trained on a bunch of 30 or 40 men who had collected between vehicles and guns with hands held high. Some of them were crawling incongruously through the sand on hands and knees.

In spite of the successful outcome of the little raid, the situation was not one which I relished. Those Germans were frightened to death at the moment, but sooner or later one of them would summon up a shred of courage and take a pot-shot at me with a Luger—unless I could keep them frightened to death. I shouted to the operator to pass me out the Tommy-gun, and when I got it I fired a couple of sharp bursts into the sand behind any Jerry who was a bit slow in joining his comrades. I yelled at them in Afrikaans and made expressive gestures with my hands. Their reaction was quite automatic . . . they reached higher than ever with their arms and fell into a solid column of fours. Some of them even beckoned to the stragglers to get a move on. Soon they were heading for our leaguer area at a shambling trot.

At this moment several men jumped out of the back of one of the lorries and ran towards my tank. They were wearing battle dress and black, tank-corp berets, and were yelling like mad. I took my earphones off to hear them. "British," they shouted "British. We're British." They stopped at the foot of the Honey and shouted again at me, still bewildered at the startling turn of events.

"We're British, sir. We were captured."

"O.K." I said grinning at them "Jump on."

They clambered on to the back and settled down among the bedding, chattering with pleasure and relief and relaxed tension.

The prisoners were still shambling off, shepherded by the other Honey, and I turned my attention to the guns. For a few seconds I contemplated hitching them all up behind the lorries and driving them back. It would have been a nice finale to the act which, I couldn't help recognising, was about 50 per cent. exhibitionism anyway. Then away to the south I saw the dark shapes appearing over the horizon, and moving quickly towards us. The race was on and I didn't intend to lose it, even if it meant losing my prisoners. Before we left I had the gunner plant a solid 37-mm. shot into each gun, aiming at the breech block. A shell landed about 40 yards away and it was quickly followed by a second, considerably nearer. It was time to go.

Now it was over, the reaction set in. As far as I was concerned the whole thing was quite purposeless if I did not get back to the South Africans all in one piece. I felt like running away as fast as possible ... back to the herd.

There were still the prisoners. I no longer had a great deal of interest in them, and found it impossible, not for the first or last time, to work up any positive feelings of dislike or enmity. My concern in getting them back was purely a matter of finishing things off adequately, of getting the signature of universal approval. But it wasn't all that important.

Shells were beginning to fall regularly, and every now and again I felt the unmistakable, breathtaking swish of an armour-piercing shot going past. We hurried after the trotting column and the other Honey. Instinctively I placed the tank so that the prisoners were between me and the enemy vehicles advancing from the south. I felt a little ashamed about this, but what the hell?

Then our Honey came to a dead stop and the engine spluttered into silence. The self-starter whirred away in short bursts of frustration and I thought immediately: "God damn and blast it, the bloody petrol."

The second Honey was moving slowly further and further away, apparently in ignorance of our plight. I told the driver to keep on trying in the hope that it may have been just a blocked feed, and then got everybody on my tank to wave their arms like mad to attract the attention of the red-moustached commander who was slipping gently, it seemed, out of my life. We were out of touch with anybody on the air who could do us any good, and all our hopes were centred in that one silhouette perched on top of a receding turret. The black shapes over our right shoulder were coming a little more purposefully across the desert floor now, but their shell-fire still seemed a bit hesitant and inaccurate. They must have wondered what the hell was going on.

The three troopers on the back co-operated enthusiastically in our efforts to attract attention. Their faces were a picture of understandable misery at the prospect of being blown to pieces by a direct hit or of being put in the bag once again. We still had a good 1,000 yards to go to the comparative safety of the South African leaguer, and I was beginning to think of walking it when I saw the other Honey stop, pause a moment or two in indecision, and then come wheeling back towards us.

When it came alongside it did not take more than a second or two to discover that neither vehicle had a tow-rope. There was nothing for it but to abandon the tank and transfer to the other one. By now the oncoming panzers were about as far from us as we were from the leaguer. We could not expect for very much longer to enjoy this rather haphazard im-munity. My 5th Tanks colleague evidently thought so, too. We were no sooner on board than he ordered full speed ahead and we roared past the column of Germans, still headed for the distant leaguer with arms in the air. It was a pity to leave them, but I was all for it. The last I saw of them was a black blob on the desert, still moving, but with their hands no longer raised. It was not difficult to imagine their conversation.

The Honey was getting near the friendly perimeter now, going hell-bent. I waited for it to slow down, and then noticed that the tank commander was looking back towards the Jerries and that any minute the vehicle would go plunging into our own lines. I yelled and bent down over the front to try and stop the driver with a hand signal. At the same time the commander must have seen the situation looming up swiftly ahead of him, and given a violent order to the driver. The Honey stopped dead in its tracks. Unfortunately, I went sailing on at about 35 miles an hour and landed with a frightful crunch on my shoulder and the side of my face, at the feet of some very puzzled anti-tank gunners. I walked into the leaguer area sore, cursing and picking bits of gravel out of my skin.

It was, no doubt, a suitable anti-climax. I felt lousy and deflated; and I was on my flat feet again, tankless. My recent crew gravitated towards me with the three escaped prisoners. I told them to try and locate their sergeant and then report to the most senior officer they could find.

"Thanks for everything," I said to them. "You've done very well. See you back at brigade one of these days."

They saluted smartly and went off looking, I thought, rather relieved. I wandered around trying to pick out a Honey in the welter of vehicles that could lead me to the Colonel and, if possible, another tank.

I found the Honeys first and then the C.O., in a small group of officers and N.C.O.s huddled over their maps. I joined them silently, but if I hoped to discover what was going on everywhere I was to be disappointed. With brief jabs of his finger the C.O. pointed to where he thought various headquarters were. 4th Armoured Brigade was scattered all over the desert; he had heard nothing of our own 'A' and 'B' Squadrons, and

5th Tanks and 8th Hussars were in more or less the same position. The general situation was equally obscure and confused, but it had been reported that there was a considerable concentration of enemy tanks and vehicles to the south and south-west of our position. General Gott, commanding 7th Armoured Division, had been personally in touch with the C.O., and we had orders to stay in the South African leaguer and assist them against any attack which might be made.

For a moment or two I considered telling them about my little episode with the field-guns, but as the first sentences formed themselves in my mind it struck me that it would sound like a hell of a line-shoot, and this was neither the time nor the place for line-shooting. We walked together down to the southern edge of the encampment, and stared across the sand and scrub to the south-west. Only the burnt-out remains of tanks and lorries and the motionless shapes of unrecognisable derelicts relieved the flat monotony. I wondered what had happened to my prisoners and to their guns, and to the tanks which had chased us off. I scanned the horizon to the west but could see no sign of them. With a proper awareness of the situation they had probably wasted no time in getting away.

There was a long, low ridge some two or three miles to the southward of where we stood, and it must have been behind this fold in the ground that the massing of enemy forces was invisibly proceeding. I looked at my watch as we broke up, and the tank commanders went back to their vehicles. I was surprised to see that the morning had gone. A strange and ominous lull drifted over the afternoon, grey under its canopy of cloud. Men moved silently between slit trenches, working shirtless to get them deeper, or sat leaning back against truck wheels eating their meagre rations. Every now and then an armoured car would move swiftly across the skyline.

I told the Colonel shortly how I had come to be without a

tank—it was news to him that I had managed to get one—
and said that I would like to have another one to go out and
try and recover mine. He let me have one of his headquarters
troop, and I had a quick meal on my new crew's biscuits and
jam. We even had a brew on a borrowed South African fire
while I practised my rusty Afrikaans. I was in no great hurry.

Just after 3 o'clock the adjutant came round our half-dozen
tanks to tell each of us that the armoured cars out in front
had reported a mass movement of the enemy towards the
leaguer area, and that an attack seemed to be imminent. Each
tank was to select a position between the anti-tank guns which
had moved into line around the southern and western peri-
meters. The only battle orders we had were to keep the enemy
out.

We climbed back into our tanks—all weary in body and
spirit, numb under the accumulating impact of events, without the energy for imagination, without the anticipation of
fear. Each Honey moved off to the spot selected by its commander. I chose a vacant space between two 2-pounders still
mounted on the backs of their portees, their crews crouched
behind the flimsy protection of the gun shield. They looked
horribly exposed on top of those vehicles, and I wondered
why they hadn't gone to ground and got properly dug-in.
From being on the receiving end, I knew only too well what
a vicious weapon a concealed, dug-in anti-tank gun can be. I
leaned over and asked them why they preferred to be on top
of their truck instead of below the surface. They grinned back
at me, and said they hadn't been in any one place more than
an hour for the past two days, and asked if I had tried to do
any digging around those parts.

"It's as rocky as hell under the top six inches," they told
me.

"Well," I grinned back. "It's none of my mucking business."

It was too late to do anything about it, anyway. We were grouped right on the south-western corner of the leaguer, facing almost due south. We had barely finished our little chat when the horizon to our front grew unsubstantial and mobile with the dark silhouettes of what looked like hundreds of vehicles. I shouted "Hier kom hulle" to my South African neighbours, and told the gunner to load both guns. Then, with touchy memories of the morning. I ordered the driver to switch off. If we had to stay there we wouldn't be needing the engine. If we had to move we would need all the petrol we could save. I felt sorry for the driver, in his silent, impotent little cabin, seeing that visible death coming towards him.

As the massed enemy drew nearer they became distinguishable as a vast array of tanks, guns and lorried infantry in what was by now a familiar battle formation—a solid, embattled column with the heavy panzers at the head of the battering ram in a ponderous phalanx of destruction, followed by the lines of tall lorries protected on flank and rear by the ranks of light tanks and armoured cars. There appeared to be 20 or 30 panzers in the leading block, and about as many other armoured vehicles in the rest of the column.

"Christ," I thought, "this is it; nothing can stop that lot. It's worse than yesterday. Yesterday I could at least run away."

They came steadily nearer—a great, black juggernaut of irresistible menace; the sombre camouflage of the tanks red-tinged as the frightened sun sank behind them. Then our artillery went into action, breaking up the solidity of the design with sudden bursts of smoke and dirt. But there was no break in the tempo or the purpose of that evil, crawling mass. We waited for the tanks to come within range of our puny guns, letting the full and horrible fascination of the sight sink indelibly into our minds, forever. To some of us 'forever' was still going to be quite a long time; to some of us 'forever' was only going to be a few more seconds.

As I watched them I became aware that the course they were on would carry them past the leaguer. They were heading north-west, and unless they changed direction they would run right across the south-western corner a good 500 yards clear. I felt a vast weight lift off my spirit. We were not going to be physically overrun by those massive tracks. We were not the real objective. Somewhere over the horizon lay the real target. The objective was still Sidi Rezegh.

It was a fleeting thought, but it lightened my darkness. We could see the gun flashes sprouting from the squat turrets, and the air grew noisy and foul as the shells started falling among us. Another full minute of dreadful inactivity as we waited for our own guns to become effective, and then 2-pounder and 37-mm. started barking back with their shriller yapping. The air was suddenly full of tracer, curving out in long rods and then cavorting up into the sky as the shot hit those thick, armoured sides.

I gave my gunner the fire order, and was momentarily startled by its familiar sound. It was exactly the same as I had given to the other gunner—how many hours and how many gunners ago?—on the airfield at Sidi Rezegh : "Thirty-seven. Enemy tanks. Stick on one until you stop it. Fire!" And I watched the red tracer screaming out as the whipcrack of the gun jarred my teeth.

"That was a hit," I told the gunner. "Stay with it."

On each side of me the South African 2-pounders were firing as fast as they could be loaded. I felt sorry for them and a little embarrassed at my own comparative security. Even as I watched, the shield in front of the right-hand gun disintegrated in slivers of steel from a direct hit, and the man sitting behind it with his eye to the telescopic sight disintegrated in slivers of flesh. Men dragged away the mutilated body, and then went back to their job. The gun went on firing for a few more shots, then the portee heaved again and two men threw up their arms and lurched off on to the sand. I got a little lower in the turret.

The enemy column was now at its closest point to the South African position, and the battle in my vicinity reached a crescendo of noise and furiousness. The mass of tanks passed steadily across our front, and the dark air was patterned with tracers and the vivid flashes of guns. Behind it all the sun had left a broad, blood red trail across the sky, bathing the desert in this ominous light, lighting up the steel sides of the panzer horde and the dark canvas of the infantry lorries with a glow straight from the fires of hell. Automatically I watched the tracers from my own gun screaming off, not curved now but hurtling in a flat line at the nearest Mark IVs. Suddenly, above the din, I heard my gunner yelling: "Got him, sir. I've got him. That's the second bastard." I saw the great black shape halt and stay immobile as the column passed on. The turret did not open and no lazy, tell-tale smoke could be seen. I watched its gun carefully through my binoculars. It was silent.

I leant down to pat the gunner and said into the mike, grinning at him: "Nice work, cock. Keep it going. You're winning the battle."

I heard the 37-mm. crack again, and almost disinterestedly I watched the tracer. The anti-tank gun on my left was still firing hard, partly protected by the Honey's armour; the one on my right was shattered and mute, and so was its crew. Subconsciously I was aware of the tumult all around and the black, smelly clouds that wafted over the tank every few seconds from a nearby shell-burst. I was hypnotised by that mass of doom moving across the flat plane of the desert. It was a feeling stronger than fear, stronger than any sort of personal sensation, as though I were some detached, uncorporate observer functioning as a tank commander by force of habit and familiar drill.

More than ever I was conscious of relief at the realisation that we were not their objective. We were an incidental obstacle; a brief encounter. 'Where the hell are they going?' I thought. 'Why don't they turn now and ride right over us?' But they went on, past the point of proximity, on into the emptiness of the north-west, away from us towards their intended engagement. Behind them they left the smoking relics of their passage, and as the great tanks churned on, the staccato rattle of machine-gun fire replaced the boom and thunder of the guns and shells. Every now and again a mushroom of flame and smoke would leap skyward as one of the lorries was set alight by a direct hit, spilling its human cargo on to the sands. At one moment there was a great orange-coloured upheaval, as the complete turret of a Mark III lifted bodily into the air from some internal explosion.

I felt a jerk on my trouser-leg, and looked down to hear the operator yelling that there was no more ammunition. Within the next few minutes the other tank commanders could all be heard telling the C.O. they had run out of ammo, and asking what were they to do about it. The reply was specific. We were to stay where we were, in the line. Nobody was to move until ordered.

It was a grim ten minutes—just sitting there in that turbulent twilight while the shells whined and crashed round, and the desert heaved and men reared up grotesquely and then lay still or twitching. But the high peak of the action had passed with the passing of the panzers, and every minute lessened the tension and the menace.

With our guns pitifully silent, fighting the enemy with static armour-plating and the moral effect of our presence on those about us, I don't think any of the Honeys would have moved out of line at that moment even if they had been allowed to. As the tempo of the battle slackened and the light dwindled with a cruel reluctance, we got our orders to pull out and rally by the colonel's tank about 100 yards back. We could just see the twin yellow pennants fluttering at the head of his wireless aerial. The order emphasised that we were to reverse very slowly out of our positions and to create as little alarm as possible. There was still plenty of stuff whizzing around, but mostly small-arms fire, and I think the less fortunate people on the ground found our continued presence some reassurance against a possible infantry attack.

I told the driver to start up, and had my usual moment of suspense and relief as the starter whirred and the engine fired. We moved back imperceptibly, but I was immediately conscious of the puzzled, angry looks on the faces of the infantrymen and gunners. I knew exactly what they were thinking and, for the sake of the tanks rather than myself, I shouted to them "Our ammo's finished. We're just pulling back to get more." Their expression changed to relief and understanding. Some of them smiled and waved or gave the thumbs-up sign. We continued to back away slowly, through the vehicles and slit trenches, past all the other worried, perplexed looks; feeling uncomfortable about it, but glad to go.

From different corners of the perimeter the meagre band of Honeys converged on the high pennants. Alongside the Colonel's tank was a lean-looking Crusader and perched on its turret studying a map was our C.O., together with a tall man in a white sheepskin jacket and a peaked cap. I recognised him as General Gott, the divisional commander. 'Poor devil,' I thought; 'what a way to have to run a battle—tearing round the desert looking for your brigades and regiments; telling each group separately what they had to do; trying to make something cohesive out of that utter confusion.' At the same time I wondered if we wouldn't all have been better off if the Generals had stayed at their posts.

A few minutes' quick conversation, and the colonel jumped down, saluting smartly as the Crusader wheeled about and snaked off into the gathering night. The C.O. beckoned us over. It was just to tell us we were to pull back into a New Zealand leaguer for the night. He couldn't satisfy our curiosity or relieve our bewilderment and fears. Apparently nobody, not even the enemy, knew what the hell was going on anywhere.

Somehow we all felt very much better at the knowledge that there were now New Zealand troops in the battle area. It was not only that it meant that here were new sources of strength which had not yet been fully committed, but from a joint experience in Greece and Crete we knew what wonderful troops they were. I know what was in my mind, and I think it was a feeling shared by all of us . . . that we would be able to get some rest during the night without fear of being massacred. We went off behind the C.O. in a much brighter frame of mind, buoyed up by the knowledge of the powerful forces still unused on our side and confident that the battle we had thought nearly lost would now be won.

In single file we moved away from the South Africans, wondering what would happen to them, hoping someone would do something about them. In the darkness we came to the New Zealanders, moving cautiously until we had cleared their outlying pickets. We were expected, and were guided to an area in which we could spend the few hours before the lightening east would disperse us again in wakefulness. My new tank crew, being in headquarters troop, were adepts at making hot tea without showing a flicker of light. That was a mug of tea! When we had finished it, too tired to be hungry and too exhausted and satiated with incident to discuss the day past or the day to come, we fell asleep where we sat or slouched.

My own few lines of immortality on Totensonntag were scribbled in German in the War Diary of 15th Panzer: "... a Batterie of Artillerie Regiment 33 was overrun by a sudden charge of English tanks and forced to surrender. The Batterie was recaptured and later brought into action again."

Much later, I hope.

Seventh Day

By 6 o'clock the Honeys were dispersed outside the New Zealand perimeter. We were rested, and we had had permission to brew up. My crew had not been used to going without a hot breakfast, and were pretty well organised to get one. They had not yet had to make one of those wild dashes for the tank leaving the kettle half-boiled and bacon just warming up as the first shell pitched into the sand or the first yell came over the air that panzers were approaching. Leaving a brew half-brewed was one of the most difficult things to do in that campaign. It was a decision often measured carefully against a shattered limb or death. There was no violent interruption this morning, and no breakfast was ever enjoyed more than that fried bacon laid on hard biscuit, followed by hot, strong tea.

At 9 o'clock a three-tonner came round to each tank and filled it up with high octane spirit. I thought of my drained-dry Honey of the previous day, and wondered what had happened to it. The first orders came over the air. We were to rejoin Headquarters, 4th Armoured Brigade, by marching six miles on a bearing of 117 degrees and a further six miles on a bearing of 158 degrees. Staff officers had obviously spent a busy night trying to get formations together again after the holocaust and disintegration of Sidi Rezegh.

The 3rd Battalion's paltry six Honeys—we were still minus 'A' and 'B' Squadrons—moved off in an easterly direction. I looked at the map resting on the turret-top in front of me, tracing our intended journey past trig. points, birs and hagfets that had now grown familiar through frequent reference.

After half an hour of uneventfulness we heard that Brigade H.Q. was on its way from the south-west, and we were to make contact at Bir el Haleizen. There, at noon, we met up once again with Brigadier Gatehouse.

From that moment on I can truthfully say that none of us had more than the vaguest idea where we were from day to day and hour to hour, or what was happening either to our own forces or the enemy's. The campaign swung violently from one end of the desert to the other. One morning we would be south-west of Sidi Rézegh; the next afternoon we would be well east of the point at which we had spent the first night after crossing The Wire. That I had actually seen the rooftops of Bardia that second afternoon was an unbelievable dream, part of another unreal existence. There was no such thing as advance and retreat. We roared off to areas of threat or engagement depending on the urgency of the information. We chased mirages and were chased by mirages. Every few hours a landmark or a name would punch our memories with an elusive familiarity, and we would recall a forgotten early incident or a battle fought there days before that was now part of a past so near in time but so distant in event.

We went without sleep, without food, without washing or change of clothes, without conversation beyond the clipped talk of wireless procedure and orders. In permanent need of everything civilised, we snatched greedily at everything we could find, getting neither enjoyment nor nourishment.

The daily formula was nearly always the same—up at any time between midnight and 4 o'clock; movement out of the leaguer into battle positions before first light; a biscuit and spoonful of marmalade before the flap of orders and information; the long day of movement and vigil and encounter, death and the fear of death, until darkness put a limit to vision and purpose on both sides; the drawing in of far-flung forma-

tions; the final endurance of the black, close-linked march to
the leaguer area; the maintenance and replenishment and
order groups that lasted till midnight; the beginning of another 24 hours.

Within this framework the battles were fought, the tanks
were knocked out, the crews killed, or maimed or fried. At
the end of each day the brief relief of the last-light pause,
when the desert grew quiet and cold and the moon rose on
the sand and scrub making black shadows of the escarpments
and moving black shadows of the funereal columns of smoke
. . . that pause had to be used to contact troop and squadron
and regiment till the long lines of Honeys and Crusaders, like
chains of dogs sniffing their introduction and recognition,
moved off nose-to-tail in the night. Deluges of sand and dust
kicked up by the tracks flooded into turrets, splashing on the
inert, shapeless forms of gunner and operator already in a
realm of unconsciousness that could never be called sleep,
showering on the tank commander, trying by reassuring
chatter over the inter-com. to keep his driver awake. They
were nightmare rides, but they had the merit of being without fear and imagined annihilation; there was always the
security of the leaguer at the end of the ride.

Most of us allayed the weariness and discomfort of those
night marches by tuning in to the B.B.C. or that Middle Euro-
pean station which, night after night, played Lili Marlene for
the benefit of the Afrika Korps and the tear-jerking nostalgia
of the Eighth Army. So the night and the snatched sleep and
the unwilling dawn.

This first day after Sidi Rezegh was to set the pattern of
many that followed. The remnants of 4th Armoured Brigade
dribbled in from all corners of the desert until it became re-
established as a fighting unit, if only at half-strength. The
3rd Battalion was still minus two squadrons which, we heard,
were swanning about somewhere with other organisations.

There was an early conference of senior officers, but not even at Brigade Headquarters could any authentic picture be created of what was happening in the battle. There seemed to be a general impression in the upper strata that Rommel and his armoured divisions had been roughly handled throughout the campaign, and that all his moves were tactical withdrawals. Whether this was a deliberately-created impression I do not know—we certainly found it difficult to believe, but we clung hopefully to the idea that it was right. It was far more likely to have been the result of misleading reports of the amount of damage and casualties inflicted on the enemy.

Gatehouse, who could not have been ignorant of the true situation, was always supremely confident simply because it was not in his nature to feel any other way. He was completely sure of himself and his ability to control any situation his forces found themselves in. It was only down at our level, in the turrets and the slit trenches, that we had our doubts. We were seldom under the impression that we had given the Germans a hell of a hiding in any of the organised encounters. Usually, we just hoped that in some other locality, in some other part of the battle, he was having a worse time than he was getting from us. Thank God, he very often was.

Our C.O. came back from that conference without the gen we were all hoping for, and we were sent scurrying out in a protective screen around Brigade H.Q. An attack was expected from the north where, apparently, large enemy forces were deploying. Over the skyline, about eight miles away, lay the landing ground of Sidi Rezegh. Already, as far as I was concerned, it was just a fantastic memory. There was just no room for it in the overcrowded present and future.

The day wore on in uneventful watchfulness, while we lay immobile. We had to struggle continually to keep awake. In mid-afternoon we were jerked into full awareness by an order to assist 5th Tanks in an attack on a large enemy column of M.E.T. which was moving south-east, about four miles from us. With my troop in the lead, we travelled about five miles in the direction indicated, but I was unable to report any visible sign of the enemy. We came to a rather straggling halt, wondering where the hell to go from there, when we got an urgent summons back to Brigade, who were again expecting an attack from the north-west. We made quick time back over our earlier track marks, to find the headquarters tanks and vehicles lying somnolent in the sun and the horizons empty of any moving threat. Another ten minutes and we were heading back east again spurred on by that now familiar-sounding phrase "a large column of enemy M.E.T. heading south-east". This time it was real enough.

A long dense line of vehicles stretched solidly across the desert, moving slowly from north to south. It looked like the Exodus. From a suitable turret-down position with only my head and shoulders and binoculars above the sky-line I scanned the column about 2,000 yards ahead. Everything was clear in detail—the dark, square shapes of the infantry lorries with heads peering curiously out of the open back, the hundreds of supply vehicles, the great, gaunt skeletons of a number of 88-mm. guns on tow, and not a tank nor an armoured car in sight. I switched the glasses back to the 88s. Their crews were mounted idly on various parts of the gun and framework and on the towing unit. They were moving slowly along with the broad mainstream of vehicles; placed as they were in the middle of the column, they clearly had no rôle other than movement. It would take them a good five minutes to get those great guns into action, and in half that time we could be running over them.

Switching the mike to the battalion frequency, I told the C.O. of the prize that lay waiting. It was clear from the orders that followed his acknowledgment that other eyes than mine were watching and other voices reporting. The brigadier had, in fact, just ordered the three tank regiments—or what was left of them—to attack in line on a broad front. Down the whole length of the German column's left flank the Honeys were marshalling, and at the signal to go we tore across the intervening desert in a manner that would have brought great joy to the Earl of Cadogan.

Harry Maegraith's Honey was alongside me, with my troop tanks on the other side, and as we plunged forward I made an encircling pincer motion with both arms to indicate to them that we should run right through the vehicles and then turn back and try and enclose them. It was an exhilarating charge. The dense mass of vehicles before us broke in panic and scattered all over the desert. Soon all our machine-guns were chattering away with vicious gossip. A great 88-mm. was lumbering along, its driver and crew looking over their shoulders with terrified faces. This type of gun had come to be our particular enemy, but I did not want to slow down to deal with it, as I was intent on the original manœuvre. As I sailed past the 88-mm. I emptied the chamber of my revolver at it, and then ducked into the turret as I saw the tanks on the opposite side of it traversing their guns to engage it.

The whole enemy column was now in full flight along its whole length. Vehicles were careering across the desert regardless of boulders and ditches, and the tanks were no longer gaining on them. I ordered my troop to turn about and shoot up everything that came past. We had a fine time for about ten minutes, and then, as the landscape gradually drained itself of fleeing transport, we swanned about picking off stragglers, shooting up abandoned lorries and chivvying the scores of dismounted Jerries who were roaming about with hands in the air. Two abandoned 88s attracted most attention. We were staggered at the size of the things; no wonder they could blow our tanks to pieces at 3,000 yards!

Harry Maegraith came on the air suddenly to tell me that

he could see a Jerry tank. We pulled up alongside each other and had a good look at it, chatting confidentially about it through the sets.

"That's a Mark IV, Harry. Shall we have a crack at it?"

"I'm game."

"Right. Then this is what we'll do. I'll swan about in front of it and keep it busy. You nip round the back and shoot it up when you get close enough. It's the only chance of knocking it out."

"O.K." said Harry, and we moved off in opposite directions.

The Mark IV was moving slowly in solitary magnificence along the forward slope of a rise just south of us. It was about 1,000 yards away, and was wandering along as though it did not know where to go or what to do—a trifle forlorn but full of menace. I ran diagonally towards it without attempting concealment, but fast enough to make the chances of being hit very remote. Straight in front of the panzer, at a distance of about 400 yards, were a number of scrub-covered sand dunes. When I reached there I planned to duck about, shoot off a few shots and generally create an alarming diversion. The German tank commander could not fail to notice me, and soon I saw the Mark IV come to a halt and the turret swing round towards my Honey. Over my right shoulder I could see Harry making a wide encircling movement, changing direction to come up on the German from behind. I saw one puff of smoke come from the muzzle swinging round with me, but I was not aware of any shot falling. Then we were in the sand dunes, and the turret of the Mark IV was pointed straight ahead. I kept on popping up in a hull-down position and letting off a quick shot with my cannon. Each time I could see Harry creeping up on the panzer. Finally, I just sat and watched, hardly daring to breathe, as I saw the Honey coming right in as though it were going to ram that panzer in the tail. A shell pitched in the sand just in front of me, and when the smoke cleared and I put my head out again Harry's tank had pulled up not 20 yards behind the Mark IV. In the same second I saw the flash from its 37-mm. muzzle, and almost immediately the German's turret flew open and a hand waved a white cloth out of the top. Then the figure of the tank commander emerged fluttering his handkerchief, followed by the rest of the crew. I reached for the mike:

"You got the bastard. Well done, Harry. Jesus, you frightened me to death."

"Thanks, Bob," he said quietly. "I'll send these blokes back to B.H.Q. and then have a look inside. There may be some of those chocolate rations."

Nearly all German tanks carried very tasty, nourishing chocolate in their emergency rations. It was our favourite loot. We were all very pleased with ourselves, elated after the depression of the previous two days. The Colonel got on the air to congratulate Harry, and then told us to start rallying on his tanks.

The Honeys of the whole Brigade were scattered all over the area, and clearly it was going to be a devil of a job getting everybody together again before dark. The sun had already set, and in the last light little groups of tanks could be seen weaving back from the western horizon, being guided in through their wireless sets by the battalion navigator. Some of the Honeys had been going flat out after the fleeing Germans for nearly an hour, and were recalled from points more than 10 miles from their start-line. It was the first time we had found so much M.E.T. so unprotected, and we wondered what had happened to the enemy's usually meticulous protective organisation on such occasions. We were to find out later that night.

Gradually individual tanks gathered into troops and troops into squadrons, forming up behind the C.O.'s tank in single

file, lined up ready on the bearing that was to take us through
the blind darkness to our leaguer area. As we waited in the
ghostly desert light for the last strays to come in, three lonely
figures appeared out of the emptiness and moved towards the
column of tanks. I gave them a shout, and they quickened
their pace towards my Honey; then, rather to my surprise,
raised their arms above their heads. They wore the long,
ankle-length dark overcoats which seemed to be general issue
to all Axis troops in North Africa, and as they drew near I
beckoned to them to climb aboard. This they did with alacrity,
and settled down on the back of my tank among the bedding
rolls and engine warmth, talking quietly among themselves.

The column started up and moved off into the night in the
customary linked chain, and as I peered out of the top of the
turret, my eyes closed to slits against the dust and sand, I got
an unpleasant feeling in the back of my head. Those three
prisoners might be armed, and if they changed their minds
about being put in the bag they could shoot me in the back,
jump off the tank and get away without anybody being much
the wiser. I didn't mind them getting away; prisoners were
always a damn nuisance to tank crews; but I didn't want to
be shot in the back of the head. I climbed out of the turret
and sat facing them with my legs dangling over the steel edge.
I hauled the tommy-gun from its rack and laid it ostenta-
tiously beside me.

No sooner had I settled down than one of the prisoners
stood up and started to take off his greatcoat—much to my
surprise, as the nights were always bitterly cold as soon as
the sun left the sky. I was even more astonished when he
leaned over and wrapped the overcoat round my bare knees.
It seemed to be a spontaneous gesture springing from God-
knows-what sort of impulse and it made me feel acutely embarrassed. I jumped to the conclusion that here were three
unfortunate Italians who had probably been waiters or valets

in civil life. We knew there were thousands of Italian troops in Libya, and we longed for a crack at their armoured division, but somehow we never seemed to be fighting anything but Germans and panzers. I knew no Italian but summoned up a "Non, non," and a couple of "Grazie or Grazias" and tried to push the coat back at him, feeling suddenly sorry for that pathetic trio and the fear and the loneliness that had brought them to me. The man protested with his hands and indicated vehemently the long trousers he was wearing and my flimsy khaki shorts. My own hands spoke back at him in refusal; then I pointed to each of them and said, loudly above the engine noise: "Italy? Italy? Italy?"

I could see the look of dismay and disgust that came over their faces. "Nein, nein," they said together, emphatically "Afrika Korps. Deutsch. Deutsch."

I made no further protest when the man wrapped me up again. "Hell's bells," I thought, "the master race."

The march back to leaguer went on interminably, and half a moon came up to fill the desert with a strange, unblinking light. The dust poured over us, and the long line of tanks expanded and contracted like a concertina on an ill-lit stage. All around us the invisible sky-line burst into spasmodic sprays of pyrotechnics, as the enemy fired clusters of white Very lights into the air, signalling recognition or seeking temporary visibility. The lights seemed to be everywhere— north, south, east, west and all the intermediate points. The desert was full of enemy.

In every Honey we were thinking the same thoughts, wondering what the hell was going on, wishing that somebody would tell us sometimes what was happening, switching our sets off the battalion frequency to the nostalgic wavelength of the B.B.C. Home Service, but hearing only a rather biassed report of the previous days happenings in the Sidi Rezegh area; thinking of the elderly men and women sitting in hotel lounges in Knightsbridge and Kensington, solemn and know-ledgable.

Late that night, with maintenance done, German chocolate eaten and the leaguer area a silent, steel-walled world peopled by shapeless slumberers and the mufflered silhouettes of sentries on the turreted ramparts, a summons came to the Colonel's tank, where we crawled under a bivvy and, over the spread maps, heard with astonishment of Rommel's dash to The Wire. It was an event that was to become the highlight of the desert war, but to us it seemed as though Rommel had gone clean off his bloody head.

We heard of the panic in the headquarters and supply areas, and were unpatriotically delighted at the thought of generals and staff officers fleeing for Alexandria or wetting themselves in slit trenches. It was the universal, if unmerited, reaction of the front-line troops at the thought of any form of disaster befalling the immunity of the rear areas. In this case we reckoned that the top command was making a complete mess of things anyway, and we could do just as well without them. We were also relieved to think that somebody else was getting the pasting and not us.

The C.O. told us that the Jerry column we had attacked that afternoon was the supply echelon for the tank forces racing up to The Wire, and we reflected with grim pleasure on the cursing that would be going on among the German tank crews when their petrol and rations failed to turn up. Our own 'B' echelon, which had somehow managed to arrive with our own supplies, brought with them the most lurid tales of the panic that had struck all the headquarters areas.

My friend Alan Moorehead, war correspondent of the *Daily Express*, was perhaps the one who best captured the atmosphere of that crazy day, in his dispatch to his paper. Alan and I had been pre-war colleagues on the *Express* together with those other great correspondents Noel Monks and

O'Dowd Gallagher. It was Alan, in fact, who had sent back a few days previously a story that "Bob Crisp has had both his legs shot off in a tank battle." It was some other Crisp.

On this particular afternoon Moorehead was in a party of newspapermen on their way to the battle area ostensibly to describe a great British victory. They were suddenly caught up in a mad and incomprehensible rush of vehicles all streaming in the opposite direction. "All day for 9 hours," wrote Moorehead, "we ran. It was the contagion of bewilderment and fear and ignorance. Rumour spread at every halt, no man had orders. Everyone had some theory, and no-one any plan beyond the frantic desire to reach his unit. We were just a few hangers-on of the battle, the ones who were most likely to panic because we had become separated from our officers and had no definite job to do. I came to understand something of the meaning of panic in this long, nervous drive. It was the unknown we were running away from, the unknown in ourselves and in the enemy. We did not know who was pursuing us, or how many, or how long they would be able to keep up the pursuit, and whether or not they would outstrip us in the end. In ourselves we did not know what to do. Had there been someone in authority to say 'Stand there. Do this and that . . .' then half our fears would have vanished."

Most of the people in authority around Moorehead and his companions at that time were doing just what he was doing. But back in the battle area—or what had been the battle area —the flap passed us by completely. We followed its course impersonally by the coloured arrows and rings on the map as though watching a blackboard exercise at O.C.T.U. And never for one moment, either on the night when we got the first reports or at any time during the next few days when the crayoned arrows prodded deeper and deeper until they penetrated Egypt, did we have the slightest feeling of uneasiness about the situation in our rear. I do not think it an exaggeration to say that our twin emotions of relief that we were not involved, and gratitude for the respite it offered us, were the strongest things we felt about Rommel's raid. We just assumed that the German commander had made one hell of a blunder and in due course would get it in the neck. Contributory to this feeling was the complete air superiority established by the Royal Air Force and the South African Air Force over the desert. It is significant that up to this eighth day I have barely mentioned activity in the air. It was going on all the time, but in the tank units we were not involved beyond the sight of occasional packs of Stukas going over to dive-bomb our supply vehicles—though 'dive-bombing' was a flattering description of the hurried passes which the Germans made in their anxiety to carry out their orders and get away again.

In my own mind I had not the slightest doubt that the Afrika Korps and its two panzer divisions had won the first major encounter at Sidi Rezegh, and that if they had stayed in command of that decisive area, they could have fought the Eighth Army to a standstill.

Eighth Day

As usual, we broke leaguer at first light, but this morning we pushed out into the half-light feeling a considerable relaxation of tension. It was the knowledge that all the German tanks in the desert were out of the area, back on the frontier, and we looked forward with some anticipation to a day in which if we encountered any enemy tanks at all, they would be Italian M13s. That was a different proposition altogether, and during the customary couple of hours' vigil waiting for full daylight most of us felt relaxed enough to make what had become a very rare hot brew.

None of us had an inkling of how near the Eighth Army commander had come to breaking off the desert battle and retiring to defensive positions along the frontier or even farther back. It is now history that the C.-in-C., General Auchinleck, arrived at Army Headquarters at the decisive moment, ordered Cunningham to continue to press the offensive and left a message for the troops which was circulated during this day and which ended: "There is only one order, attack and pursue. All out everyone." These top-ranking exhortations, like half-time pep talks in an inter-school rugger match, usually get a pretty ribald reception at the other end. There is such a vast difference in the circumstances surrounding the sender and the receiver. In this case most of the panic was at headquarters; the forward troops were unaware of any crisis that was worse on that day than any other day, and Auchinleck's message, if it did anything at all, only served to increase bewilderment and unease.

By this eighth day, although still a troop commander, I

was being given more and more of a free hand by the C.O., who frequently allowed me to swan off into the desert with my three troop tanks. This was not a question of lack of control on his part. He still had fewer than a dozen tanks under command; and he had come to appreciate that in view of the way this campaign was being fought, independent action, in the event of breakdown of overall direction from the top, was one way of achieving results, however localised or limited. I think he recognised, too, that I functioned best when free from restraint.

The fact that the battalion was still minus two squadrons contributed towards my freedom—though I had been put nominally under command of the 'A' Squadron major who, with the Colonel, was the only officer of field rank left. An unpleasant situation was developing between these two. There was a natural clash of temperament and character which found its outlet in repeated petty squabbles which were vented publicly over the battalion wireless.

On this particular morning I had been pushed out well forward of H.Q., and was wandering about in the usual reconnaissance rôle, trying to get as far away from authority as possible. I heard my major come on the air to me and ask for information. I switched my set to send and gave him a negative reply and my rough position. This brought no acknowledgment, and after another try without success I realised that although I could hear him and all the other battalion tanks perfectly my set was unable to transmit with sufficient strength for them to hear me. It had a very weak signal and, possibly, I was farther away from H.Q. than I had thought.

Pretty soon the cool, morning air was being warmed up by some explosive, field-rank phrases asking me what the bloody hell I thought I was doing, why didn't I acknowledge his signals, why didn't I obey orders to return, etc., etc. While this was pulverising my ears I had spotted a convoy of some

40 or 50 soft-skinned vehicles parked in open formation not
far south of me. I thought I would give this a little closer
inspection before returning to H.Q. I heard the major calling
the C.O.: "That bloody man Bob has buggered off again. He
won't answer my signals. Why the bloody hell don't you keep
him under proper control?"

Then I heard the C.O. saying, surprisingly gently in the
circumstances: "Hullo SABO, JUMO calling. Don't worry
about Bob. He can look after himself. JUMO to SABO off."

I was delighted at my inadvertent eavesdropping; when I
looked down into the turret to see the reaction, the operator
looked up at me, grinning, and gave a large wink. I tried hard
not to wink back.

In the meantime we had all been examining the still-
stationary convoy through our binoculars. There were no
tanks with them, and as far as could be seen, no anti-tank
guns. But which side did they belong to—British, German or
Italian? I had the impression that it was an enemy supply
column with a number of captured 3-tonners. I looked across
at my troop sergeant in a Honey about twenty yards away.
He picked up his mike and said that he thought they were
Jerry but wasn't sure. There was only one way of finding
out . . . by going over to them. If they were British they ought
to know what a Honey looked like, and if they started running we would know they were enemy.

Signalling to my other two tanks to conform, I gave the
driver the order to advance, and we started towards the convoy, keeping well exposed and moving slowly so as not to
start a spontaneous, panic rush. We had travelled not more
than 200 yards when the lorries nearest us suddenly started
moving, gathering speed at a rate that showed that already
they were in a flap. It was like coming suddenly upon a flock
of grazing sheep or ducks. Fear spread from truck to truck
and lorry to lorry almost telepathically, translating itself

into an immediate desire to run with the herd. In a few seconds the whole mass of transport was hurtling across the desert in full flight.

At the first sign of this movement I had given the order to speed up. It was the confirmation we needed; and as the drivers pressed down on the accelerators and the Honeys surged forward, we opened fire with our machine guns indiscriminately at the fleeing vehicles. They were at a disadvantage from their standing start and we were soon upsides with the nearest ones. I ran my Honey alongside the flank, trying to turn them in real cowboy round-up fashion. The troop followed me in single file, and I could see the turrets swivel and the Brownings spitting lead.

Suddenly the driver of a truck I was passing leaned out and waved a white handkerchief. To my horror he was wearing a battledress and black beret. I yelled at my gunner to cease fire and at the driver to halt. Then I screamed at the sergeant and corporal behind me. Some sort of noise must have penetrated their minds—they could not possibly have heard me—and they looked towards me as I waved my hands violently in a sort of wash-out signal. They realised quickly what the situation was, and we pulled up in a rather crestfallen group as the nearest line of lorries stopped and the crews got down from their cabs.

I jumped down from the tank as I saw an officer coming from one of the trucks. Here we go, I thought; and I prepared to meet the verbal onslaught. He came quickly towards me with his hand stretched out and broad grin all over his face.

"Christ," he said. "Am I glad to see you! I thought we had had it this time."

"Hell's bells, man," I said, much relieved, "why did you pack up and run for it like that? Surely you could see . . ."

"After yesterday we don't wait to identify anything. We

just assume they're enemy. As soon as we see a tank we're off. We've been rushing everywhichway around this mucking desert ever since yesterday morning. We haven't a clue where our own people are. You've never seen such an imperial flap."

"I'm terribly sorry," I said genuinely, "but you know how it is. About the only way we can tell one lot of M.E.T. from another is the way they behave when they see us. I hope to hell we haven't done any damage."

"Don't worry about that. We don't blame you. In fact, it's such a relief to know that you're not Jerries that I couldn't care less about the damage."

We shook hands and left each other. His convoy was strung out across the sand and scrub, most of the vehicles halted, but some of the more distant ones were still heading for the east. As the three tanks moved off, I thought to myself what a rotten sort of life it must be in a 'B' echelon like that: living naked in a world in which everything was an enemy until it proved friendly and everything was stronger; finding protection only in flight, without power of retaliation. I wondered which was the less reassuring prospect . . . capture and the long years behind barbed wire, or always-imminent death or mutilation. I couldn't make up my mind, but nothing would have induced me to change places with that supply officer.

We got back to the battalion and a mild rocket from the Colonel for not maintaining contact. He accepted my explanation, though I made no mention of overhearing his conversation on the air.

The morning was still young, when, once more, we got an urgent summons to go to the assistance of the South African Brigade lying at Taieb el Esem. This was Dan Pienaar's outfit. In an earnest effort to deceive the enemy, it was referred to as "the boys belonging to Uncle George's nephew". General

Brink, commanding the South African Division in Egypt, was known universally as Uncle George.

The whole brigade moved off on a bearing that would bring us out on the north flank of the South Africans where, apparently, they had been under constant attack from enemy tank formations all the morning. My troop was out in front on the centre line, and at 10.30 I was able to report a large force of tanks in the distance ahead of me. On getting closer I was very relieved to see that they were the M.13s of the Italian Ariete division.

Behind me the brigade took up a battle position along a low crest facing west, while I was sent forward to find out what I could about the enemy's movements. Leaving my troop tanks behind, I pushed forward cautiously through some undulating ground which afforded good cover until I had got within about 600 yards of the Italians. Behind me the Honeys of the battalion were completely out of sight. I settled into a turret-down position, and studied the proceedings in front of me. It was quite a sight.

About 70 M13s were lined up abreast on the forward slope and crest of a long ridge that ran north and south. They stood there apparently lifeless, about 20 yards apart, their turrets firmly closed, and all facing east in the directions of 4th Armoured, whose arrival they had no doubt noticed.

It didn't look like a battle position, and it certainly didn't look as though the Italians were about to attack anything. I wondered what the idea was. Then I spotted a big lorry moving along slowly a couple of hundred yards behind the row of tanks. One by one, starting from the left of their line, they broke away and went back to the lorry, where I could plainly see men passing out jerricans of fuel and replenishing the tank. As each tank was filled up it came back to the silent line and another took its place. As soon as I realised what was happening, I yelled for artillery fire and told my C.O. to send up an O.P. from the battery of R.H.A. 25-pounders. It was a wonderful target for the guns; but it was more than that. If taken swiftly it was a wonderful opportunity to wrap up a more or less immobile Italian armoured division. I could do no more than indicate this to the higher command behind me. Personally, I had had more than enough of taking on 70 enemy tanks single-handed—even Italian tanks.

Very soon I saw the small dot of the O.P.'s Honey coming across the empty space towards me. I hoped he would use his head and take precautions that would not attract attention to the place where I was so snugly tucked in. I need not have worried. He came up alongside me without raising a wisp of dust and soon had his guns on the target.

It was good shooting, but there was never enough of it. Every gun in the area, plus a couple of visits from the R.A.F., followed up by a tank attack would have knocked Ariete right out of the war. As it was the M13s continued to refuel, not without damage, but miraculously the petrol lorry escaped obliteration and I could not but admire the way those despised Italians carried on with their job under heavy shell fire. Once a small ambulance came speeding along the row of tanks. It stopped alongside one; I saw the turret open, and an inert figure was passed down to the stretcher-bearers, who placed it in the ambulance and then drove off again.

For five hours we lay behind that ridge watching the performance. My legs were aching with continual standing; my eyes were aching with the strain of continuous watching through binoculars; and my voice was croaking with the flow of information I was sending back every few minutes. For five hours the 4th Armoured Brigade did nothing, the 7th Armoured Division did nothing, the South African Brigade a mile or two to the South did nothing. At half-past four, their refuelling completed, the Italian tanks broke off in groups of eight or ten and moved off to the north-east, pur-

sued only by the shells of our 25-pounders. In a few minutes
the ridge in front of me that had been packed with tanks, was
completely deserted. I and the O.P. turned about and went
leisurely back to our respective headquarters.

It was a disappointing occasion, but for my tank crew not
unrestful. They dozed and ate all through the day—something they had not been able to do since the first crossing of
The Wire. We lacked only a cup or two of hot tea; there was
too much risk of revealing our position and disturbing our
serenity. The Brigadier sent me a special message of thanks
for the very complete picture of enemy movements that had
been supplied. He might just as well have hung it on the wall.

That night in leaguer, near the northern face of the South
African area, one of the missing squadrons at last got in touch
with the battalion H.Q. Its commander reported that for the
past two days they had been operating with 22nd Armoured
Brigade, and hoped to rejoin in a day or two. We hoped he'd
come soon; we could do with a few extra tanks.

Ninth Day

W E could hardly believe our ears when the orders came round the leaguer just before the dawn break-up. After a short move to the flank of Pienaar's brigade we were to do nothing except tank maintenance and "personal repairs". Unless, of course, we were attacked during the course of the day. It was emphasised that our rôle was purely defensive and we were to take up a position between the South Africans and enemy tank forces in the north, more as a gesture of reassurance than anything else. Uncle George's nephew's boys seemed to be developing a pronounced panzer allergy—and who could blame them?

Thus at 6 o'clock we pushed off blithely on the half-hour's run to the new map reference figure. There the clear morning air was soon smeared by the quick spirals of black smoke from scores of petrol fires as every tank crew brewed up for breakfast and the subsequent luxury of hot water for washing and shaving.

As soon as the sun had risen high enough to generate a little warmth, we peeled off shirts, trousers, vests, underpants and socks and let the clean air lap around our bodies. It was the first time most of us had been able to take off anything for eight days—apart from essential services—and it was unbelievably refreshing to stand there naked in the sunlight and wash. The bliss of clean clothes after the mummifying effect of eight days of ever closer, smellier and dirtier confinement has to be experienced to be fully appreciated.

Then came the business of shaving a week's matted growth of beard. This was far from pleasant. The water that was pumped out from below the desert back at Sidi Barrani or Matruh was as hard and unyielding to soap as a piece of chalk. It was almost impossible to produce a lather, and shaving was a matter of hacking through the undergrowth with a succession of blades. Our skin, too, was cracked and tender from the dry, bitter winds and the extremes of temperature fluctuating between mid-day's heat and midnight's freeze.

The whole operation of washing-up had to be carefully organised in the prevailing scarcity of water. After the stand-up bath and shave it was the turn of our cast-off clothing, which we filled with soapy water as best as we could and pulverised on the nearest rock. Thereafter the desert scrub bloomed with fantastic patterns of clothing of various hues and dimensions. Any high-soaring enemy reconnaissance pilot would have had some bewildering pictures to decipher had he passed overhead that morning.

Always last to enjoy any of the rare relaxations that came our way were the tank drivers. At night, when the tanks stood in their mute rows and the crews were silent in sleep and exhaustion, grimy drivers would be seen going over the engines and tracks. In the morning's darkness they would be the first up to get their Honeys ready for the move. Their personal battle consisted in keeping their tanks mobile. An immobile tank could mean death for all. It was reasonable, no doubt, that they should have last access to the water and soap and towels: they were always covered in grease and oil and an abrasive amalgam of sand.

By midday the battalion was washed. The psychological magic of it moved us right out of the desert and its battles into some oasis of the mind in which just being able to wash and change our underclothes produced as complete a metamorphosis as being suddenly transposed to breakfast in bed in a luxury hotel with some beautiful shape filling the blankets alongside with delicious convolutions. Most of us would have settled just for the breakfast in bed.

I unrolled my valise and sleeping bag, picking out the odd bits of shrapnel that always found their way in, and lay down in the sun on my back. All round, the desert was full of leisure and relaxation and the war was far, far away. We could just hear its distant rumbles where the struggle to open the corridor to Tobruk was in progress.

Lying flat on their stomachs or propped up on one elbow, torsos naked, all the troops seemed to be writing letters:

"Dear Lil, There hasn't been much time for letters lately. I'm not allowed to tell you where we are but I've just been washing the *sand* out of my hair, the first wash for eight days. Blimey, the smell. Poor old Herb copped it the other day. I suppose his folks know by now. I helped to dig the hole. . . ."

My crew spent some time discussing plans for lunch. We settled for some bully beef pudding, a precious can of potatoes, tinned pears and condensed milk, and hot tea. I watched them making the pastry by crushing up biscuits to a fine powder, adding water and kneading it into dough. This they wrapped around the unbroken chunk of bully and placed it into one of the desert ovens they were adept at making out of sand and tin. We lay there savouring the strange smell of cooking, the saliva of anticipation trickling round our mouths. As soon as the food was hot, we ate it. A meal only needed to be hot to be different and wonderful. It felt like some long-forgotten picnic on the sands. Only the happy noise of children was missing.

C.O.'s orders were at 1.30. I rubbed the scanty aftermath of the meal off the plates in the clean sand and strolled over with Maegraith to the Colonel's tank. There we were delighted to see again the familiar face and figure of Doc MacMillan, the Medical Officer, who had disappeared with the C.O.'s staff car in the general confusion of Sidi Rezegh and

Rommel's dash to The Wire. Mac, after Calais and Greece, was something of a regimental institution, and we did not want to lose him.

The Colonel told us that twelve new Honeys were coming up for us that afternoon with Cyril Joly, who, at that time, was commanding our 'B' Echelon party but later came to my squadron. Years after, he was to write a very fine novel about the desert war. The new arrivals would bring the strength of the battalion up to 22 tanks which would be reorganised as follows: Headquarters troop, 3 tanks; 'A' Squadron, 9 tanks; 'C' Squadron, 10 tanks. "And 'C' Squadron," said the Colonel, "will be commanded by Captain Crisp."

I felt like a two-and-a-half stripe naval officer being given his first frigate. I knew it would only last until our other two squadrons with their more senior officers rejoined, but I was delighted at the opportunity and the demonstration of confidence. Maegraith was obviously very pleased, and I immediately appointed him temporary, acting, unpaid second-in-command. Our moment of glory was destined to be brief.

In the early afternoon we moved to Bir Berraneb, the favourite leaguering and mustering area of the brigade, where the newly-arrived Honeys were apportioned to the battalions. Cyril Joly came over with a flock of a dozen of them, and while the technical sergeant and his men inspected them and the new crews checked guns and equipment, the officers concentrated on the Mess lorry, which had made its first appearance of the campaign and in which we found a crate of beer that had somehow survived the war and the mad to-and-fro rushes across the desert. It made the atmosphere of holiday complete.

The supply story of the Crusader Operation would need a separate book to do it full justice in all its aspects. Every 'B' Echelon, setting off from the rear areas in its daily or nightly search for the rendezvous with its fighting echelon, had its regular encounter with the unexpected. The previous night our own replenishment column had failed to arrive, and Joly gave us the first news of what had happened to it.

It had set off from base with the rest of the Brigade transport on its routine night run to the leaguer area. In the darkness it had gone off its bearing, and had become completely detached from the other echelons. In the leading vehicle the officer in command had wisely decided not to risk his hunches and to stay where he was for the night, since the whole area was full of German columns swarming towards the frontier in the tracks of the panzer regiments. At first light he lined his truck on a bearing that he hoped would take him to the brigade leaguer, formed the convoy nose-to-tail behind him and set off into the gathering light. All round him he could see other vehicle convoys, some stationary where the night had held them captive, others moving eastwards. There was no way of telling friend from enemy, but he was able to console himself with the thought that everybody was in the same predicament and there was no reason why he should be any more frightened of them than they were of him.

Three armoured cars came up alongside the column out of the half-light, and moved parallel with it about a hundred yards on the flank. They took no other action; the officer in the truck accepted that they were friendly and felt reassured and grateful for their escort. Then one of the armoured cars moved forward across the front of the convoy, whose commander gave a cheery wave to the man poking out of the top of the turret. The man gave him a cheery wave back, and then rather surprisingly halted the armoured car slap in the path of the leading truck. The driver jammed on the brakes; the officer leaned out of the side door and was just about to let go a few well-chosen phrases when he saw the turret swinging steadily round until he found himself looking straight down the muzzles of an assortment of guns. The man on top of the armoured car grinned down and said gutturally: "Good morning. You are surprised to see me, yes?" And put the whole convoy in the bag.

We finished the beer while we listened to Cyril Joly and his description of the big flap of the previous day, to go down in the history of the Eighth Army as the Matruh Stakes. Dusk was falling, and war was present only in the distant rumble of gunfire away to the north-west.

With most of us belching merrily, the C.O. gave us the latest gen from Brigade, most of which seemed to be good. We went back to our tanks replete, refreshed and reassured —quietly happy in the knowledge that the war was being won without any undue risk to ourselves. We stayed awake long enough to hear the B.B.C. nine o'clock news, and went peacefully to sleep—much too peacefully for my well-tried philosophy that every action has an equal and opposite reaction.

Tenth Day

WHEN the message came round after morning dispersal that all squadron commanders were to attend a brigade conference at 0900 hours, it took a few minutes before I realised it was meant for me. I pulled Maegraith's leg a bit over a leisurely breakfast in which our two tank crews had joined forces in preparing something as near as we could get to a traditional eggs and bacon, toast and tea. Without the eggs.

"You'll be in command while I'm away, Harry. Senior officers' conference. Good opportunity for you youngsters to show your worth. Don't make a balls-up of the washing-up while I'm away."

Alec Gatehouse met us at his command tank. He was as usual imperturbable, solidly impressive, full of an inspiring self-confidence. Briefly he put us in the picture: 7th Armoured Brigade had gone back to railhead; 22nd Armoured had spent a day salvaging tanks and brought its strength up to 42; 4th Armoured, thanks to the recent reinforcements and the stragglers which were coming in in dribs and drabs, totalled 77 Honeys—so that the 119 tanks of various shapes and sizes of the two brigades represented the total armoured strength of 30 Corps, which had begun the battle nine days before with about 600 tanks.

Then came the real stop press news . . . General Cunningham had been relieved of his command of the Eighth Army, and had been replaced by General Ritchie. This was a shock to all of us, but not really a surprise. Even right down at the bottom of the ladder, it was impossible not to be aware of the absence of firm direction and purpose from above. Everybody welcomed the change as the beginning of an era of greater decisiveness. Nobody had ever heard of Ritchie.

With revived hope and interest, we turned to the maps laid out ready for the conference. Gatehouse quickly jabbed out the battle positions with his finger, while his crisp voice explained the crayonned formations and dispositions. We were only vaguely interested in the situation on the frontier, as it was generally accepted that Rommel couldn't be serious in his adventures in that area (we were wrong), and that the decision would still have to be fought out south of Tobruk ... with us.

The brigadier's black-haired finger traversed in one jump the embattled desert between The Wire and the Tobruk perimeter, translating the thunder and smoke of the previous evening into the rings and arrows of the British capture of the Ed Duda feature by the sortie from Tobruk. The New Zealanders were at Belhamed, separated from the garrison by a few miles and a mixed German and Italian force. The corridor into Tobruk would soon be opened and the long siege raised.

Rommel's panzer divisions were on their way back from our rear areas, having had a pretty rough time of it, though nobody knew whether they were in retreat and trying to break out to the west or rushing back to restore the position at Sidi Rezegh, which was now again dominated by the British. Orders issued by the Eighth Army plainly indicated their uncertainty of the enemy intentions. 4th Armoured Brigade had been given two alternative rôles for the immediate future. The first was to stay in the area we now occupied, prepared to engage any enemy column within a radius of 30 miles; the second was to be ready to advance to a battle position south of Acroma away to the west of the battle area. The second plan meant clearly that Rommel would be pulling out beaten. It was a nice thought, but we didn't believe it. Not yet. But it would make good telling to the tired tank crews. We were all getting to the stage where a few straws to grab hold of came in handy.

Back at the squadron I found that new officers and crews had come up with the replenishment vehicles, and after I had given out the gen, the morning was spent reorganising tank crews and rushing through drill and troop tactics. One young officer assigned to 'C' Squadron had arrived in the Middle East from England only seven days before. I told him that the main thing I wanted him to do when we got into a scrap was to conform to my movements—keep up alongside me and make the troop keep up alongside him. Then I told them the few imperative do's and dont's which I had already discovered were essential to survival in tank warfare.

I was in the middle of showing them elementary troop movements with a few pebbles in the sand when my wireless operator yelled: "Sir! The C.O. wants you urgently." I ran across to the Honey, where the operator handed me down earphones and mike. It was an order for the whole brigade to move north-east to the Trigh Capuzzo to assist 22nd Armoured in an attack on an enemy column of 2,000 vehicles, including 50 to 60 tanks. I passed on the orders to the tank commanders grouped conveniently nearby, and told them to get mounted and start up. It looked like another mad charge, and my parting words to the new boys were: "Listen. This is your first battle. It will probably end up in complete confusion. Keep your eyes on my Honey all the time. Know where it is all the time and conform to its movements. We'll move up to that ridge line abreast. Stay turret-down—not hull-down, turret-down—until I give the signal to move. Got it? O.K. See you at suppertime."

Officers and crews ran over to their tanks, and soon the air was filled with the roaring of engines as the drivers started

up and revved the radials. I had split my ten Honeys into
three troops of three with Maegraith in command of one and
the two new officers leading the others. As we ran up the long
slope of the ridge I saw the tanks spread out on either side of
me in a long straight line with about 40 yards between each
vehicle. Well over on my left "A" Squadron were beginning
the same manœuvre, while beyond them, and out of our
vision, 5th Tanks would be doing something similar—and so
right along the ridge flanking the Trigh Capuzzo to the
furthermost Crusader of 22nd Armoured Brigade, whose job
it was to hit the head of the German column while we climbed
into the flank and rear.

As my Honey edged up to the final crest I was immediately
aware of the dense throng of transport in front of me. The
Trigh was black and broad and moving with packed trucks
and lorries. Over it all hung a thick, drifting fog of dust so
that only the nearest stream of vehicles was clearly discernible. There was not a panzer in sight. The tail of the
enemy column was just on our right front, and it looked as
though we could not have timed it better. The Germans gave
no sign of having seen us, or of being aware of our tanks
poised for the strike within a thousand yards of them. They
moved slowly westwards wondering, no doubt, what the
devil Rommel thought he was playing at with these mad
rushes up and down the desert, and beefing like hell about the
dust.

I looked approvingly to right and left, where the rest of
the squadron were lined up following the curve of the con-
tour. From each turret top poked the head and shoulders of
the commander, eyes glued to binoculars trained on that
enemy mass. It must have been quite a sight to somebody only
a week out from base camp in England. I got on the air to
the C.O. with a quick, formal announcement that 'C' Squadron
was in position and ready. From my left the other squadron

did the same. Within a minute the reply came: "Hullo JAGO, JAGO calling. Attack now. Alec sends a special message 'Go like hell and good luck'. Good luck from me too. JAGO to JAGO, off."

The order went through all the intercoms. from commander to crew: "Driver, advance. Speed up. Gunner, load both guns." The Honeys positively leapt over the top of the ridge and plunged down the steady incline to the Trigh. I knew my driver, who was getting used to this sort of thing, would have his foot hard down on the accelerator, straining his eyes through the narrow slit before him to avoid the sudden outcrops of rock or the slit trenches that littered this oft-contested terrain. On each side the Honeys were up level with me. That was good. My wrist-watch showed 1 o'clock as I gripped hard on the edge of the cupola and pressed back against the side to ride the bucking tank.

We were half-way down the slope and going like bats out of hell in the bright sunlight before the Jerries realised what was happening. Then the familiar pattern of alarm and confusion and panic-flight away from us at right angles to the road. There was no slackening of speed, and within another minute we had hit the soft sand of the well-worn desert highway and become absorbed into the cloud of dust and that frightened herd of vehicles stampeding blindly northwards.

I had the same intention in my mind as on a previous occasion—to go right through them, turn about and cut off as many as possible, shooting up everything that tried to get past. I put the mike close to my lips and told my tank commanders briefly to start shooting. My own gunner pulled the trigger immediately and within seconds the dust was full of the criss-cross pattern of tracers drawing red lines through the yellow cloud and puncturing the fleeing dark shapes with deadly points. From the turret tops we let go with tommy-guns and revolvers, and every now and again the whip-crack of the 37-mm. interjected the staccato chatter of the Brown-ings. I could still see a Honey or two racing alongside, but what was happening beyond the narrow limits of vision I could only guess. And my guess was that the whole squadron was there. Another minute perhaps, I thought, and then I would give the order to turn about.

Suddenly, through the dust, I saw the flat plane of the ground disappear into space. I yelled like mad at the driver to halt. He had seen the danger only a fraction of a second after I had, and jerked back on the brakes even while I was shouting at him. The tracks locked fast and tore up sand, rock and scrub in a brief and frantic tussle to stop the momentum of the tank. We skidded to a violent stop with the front sprockets hanging over a sharp drop that started the descent of a steep escarpment.

The first thing I saw, through popping eyes, ten yards in front and below me, was a motor-cycle combination lying on its side with three German soldiers standing stiffly at atten-tion in a row beside it, their backs towards me and their hands stretched high above their heads. I rejected immedi-ately a quick impulse to shoot them. While my mind was still trying to absorb this apparition I became aware of the astonishing scene at the foot of the escarpment, where it levelled out into a broad wadi. Vehicles of all shapes and sizes were everywhere—some upright and still moving away as fast as they could; others stationary and bewildered; many lying on their sides or backs with wheels poking grotesquely upwards. Dark figures of men darted wildly about.

Even as I watched, a great lorry went plunging down the escarpment out of control; it struck some outcrop and leapt high into the air, somersaulting to the bottom in a fantastic avalanche of earth, rock and scrub and odd-shaped bundles of men integrated with jagged pieces of wood and metal. The concentration of transport in the wadi below was a wonderful target. I said quickly into the mouthpiece: "Both guns. Men and vehicles. Fire with everything you've got."

The bullets went zipping inches above the heads of the three immovable figures in front of the tank. They never twitched a muscle. When the 37-mm. cannon suddenly went off they jumped involuntarily, but none of them turned their heads or gave any indication that I could see of fear or curiosity. They just stood there, three backs and three pairs of arms while the tracers went streaming in flat, straight lines into the dusty turmoil below. I wondered idly where the rest of the Honeys were, and if they were having as good a time as mine was.

Suddenly there was a fearful bang, and simultaneously I was drenched from head to foot in an astonishing cascade of cold water. For a moment or two I was physically and mentally paralysed. I just could not believe that anything like that could happen. Then realisation came swiftly and terribly . . . the water tins on the back of the tank had been hit. It could mean only one thing. As I looked backwards I was already giving the order to the gunner to traverse the turret as fast as he bloody well could. In one comprehensive flash I saw it all, and the fear leapt up in me. Not fifty yards away a 50-mm. anti-tank gun pointed straight at the Honey, pointed straight between my eyes. Beyond it were other guns and then as the dust drifted over the scarp the sight I had dreaded most—a number of motionless Honeys and the huddled figures of black-bereted men crouched on the sand or stretched out in the agony of death.

It took less than a second for the whole scene and its awful meaning to register in my mind. I could see the German gunners slamming the next shell into the breech as the turret whirled. I yelled "On. Machine gun. Fire." In the same moment I saw the puff of smoke from the anti-tank gun and felt and heard the strike on the armour-plating. Quickly I looked down into the turret. A foot or two below me the gunner was staring at his hand, over which a dark red stain was slowly spreading. Then he gave a scream and fell grovelling on the floor. In the top right hand corner of the turret a jagged hole gaped, and through it, like some macabre peepshow, I could see the gun being reloaded. I knew that in another few seconds I would be dead, but something well beyond reason or sanity impelled my muscles and actions.

I leaned down and pulled the trigger, and kept my finger there until the gun jammed. God knows where the bullets went. Twice I felt the Honey shudder and the second time more water came pouring in. When the Browning stopped and my mind leapt about searching for some way to stay alive I suddenly saw the slim chance. If the tank would move at all, and we could drop over the edge of the escarpment, we would be out of sight of those blasted anti-tank guns. I could see them framed in that jagged hole, the gunners working feverishly, their faces strained and vicious. I said urgently into the mike: "Driver, advance. Over the edge. Quick!"

Nothing. I thought "My God, Whaley's had it. We've all had it," and screamed down into the turret "Driver, advance. For Christ's sake advance!" Then I saw what had happened. In falling, the gunner had jerked back on the intercom leads to the driver's earphones. The cords had tightened round his neck, pulling him backwards over the driving seat and half-strangling him. He wrestled frantically with his earphones and ripped them off. He didn't need them to hear my panic bellowing.

I felt the gears engage, and for a split second the world stood still. Then the engine revved, and the Honey heaved forward and dropped with a violent crash over the escarpment. In the turret we were hurled about like corks, and then

the bouncing stopped and we rode smoothly down the slope.
We were out of sight of the guns on top of the escarpment,
and with a great rush of unbelief I knew we were going to get
away with it. The three German motor-cyclists still stood
motionless. The tank could not have missed them by more
than a few inches, yet they still had their hands in the air.
Down in the driving compartment Whaley was wrestling with
the sticks to keep the tank on a diagonal course that would
take him to the bottom of the slope away from the enemy.
When the ground levelled out a bit I ordered him to turn right
to run into a little wadi that offered a safe way out to the
south. We were travelling with the turret back to front, and
I prodded the operator with my foot as he bent over the pros-
trate gunner and indicated to him that I wanted the turret
traversed back to the normal position. While he was turning
the handle I could not resist a last backward look at those
three men. Incredibly, they were still standing as we had left
them. I began to think they had become literally petrified
with fright and would stay there down the centuries in some
miraculous monument.

So much had happened in a few minutes, or a few hours it
might have been, and I had looked so closely into the valley
of the shadow, that I found it difficult to return to reality. I
just could not fully absorb our situation. I had to grip the
hardness of the armour-plating and see the familiar figures of
the tank crew to realise that we were still alive, and that we
were going to stay alive. The gunner lay there groaning in
pain and sobbing in fear. There was nothing much wrong with
him, and I shouted at him roughly to pull himself together.
My thoughts went out to the rest of the squadron. Where were
they? What had happened to them? Were they all dead? It
was something I had to find out.

We were chugging along casually through the deserted

silence of the wadi. It was uncanny after the tumult and terror just behind us, and the thought kept on intruding that we were no longer on earth, that we were driving in some ghost tank on another level of existence . . . that we were all dead. When I put the mouthpiece to my lips I was half-prepared to hear no voice come out. The unreality persisted when the Honey swung right in response to my order, and moved slowly up the slope to the crest. As soon as my eyes were above the lip of the escarpment we halted, and the full picture of horror burst on me immediately.

Not much more than 500 yards away, like a projection on a cinema screen, lay the battlefield. My eyes lifted to the tall black columns, leaning slightly with the wind, and followed them down to the Honeys gasping smoke. Four of my tanks were blazing infernos; three others just sat there, sad and abandoned. A line of anti-tank guns with their crews still manning them expectantly, lined the edge of the drop. The whole scene was silhouetted sharply against the yellow clouds of dust which rose in a thick fog from the wadi below. I could see many men running about between guns and tanks and vehicles. My heart ached as I picked out the familiar beretted figures of our own troops, huddled in disconsolate groups or being shepherded singly by gesticulating Germans.

Was there nothing I could do? My mind moved round the prospect of a sudden charge into that line of anti-tank guns, over-running them before they could get their sights on me. If I had had a gunner to fire the Browning, perhaps I might have. As it was I was grateful for the opportunity of rejecting it as impossible, and so prolonging my life and those of my crew. But who knows? It might have come off.

As a concession to my own great distress and impotency I stood up on the turret and waved my beret. There was a chance that some gunner, operator or driver, one of the commanders perhaps, might have been lying crouched in the scrub, waiting for the night or the unbidden moment to make a break for it. But it was more of a gesture of complete despair, and when I heard the whishing past my ears, followed by the quick barking of the machine guns, I dropped back into the turret. I said wearily over the intercom: "O.K., Whaley. There's nothing we can do. Let's go back."

We followed the wadi southwards as it grew shallower and shallower, eventually disgorging us unobtrusively on to the plateau over which we had charged so bravely . . . when? ten minutes ago? an hour ago? today? yesterday? and how many lives ago? My wrist-watch was staring me in the face as we paused on the rim of the depression. The hands pointed to 17 minutes past one. 17 minutes.

In the middle distance I saw something moving through the scrub. It was a Honey, and I steered Whaley towards it. Soon, its commander spotted me and altered course to come alongside. Unbelievably I recognised Harry Maegraith in the turret. He jumped down and ran across.

"Bob, I'm bloody sorry. I got a petrol stoppage half-way down the slope. I saw you all disappearing into those Jerries. What's happened?"

Incoherently, fighting the emotion that filled my chest and throat, I tried to tell him the story of the past few minutes. The words gushed out violently, bringing with them as I re-created the scene a full realisation of its meaning. Uncontrollable sobs tore my sentences into barely articulate phrases.

"Where are all the other tanks? They should have been up there. Where are they?"

"They didn't go in with you, Bob. They were swanning about on the road the last time I saw them."

"The bastards. The mucking bastards." I beat the hard armour plating with my fists. Harry, standing beside me, slipped his arm around my shoulders.

"Take it easy, Bob. Take it easy," he said, gently. "Are you sure you feel all right? There's blood all over your face."

It was a surprising bit of information, and I passed a hand across my forehead to feel the gritty lines of dried blood.

"I'm all right. It must be somebody else's. My gunner is hit. We'd better get him back. There's nothing we can do here."

We moved off together, back across the Trigh and up the long slope. I could not shake off the black mood of anger and despair. On the crest of the ridge I saw the silhouette of a tank and veered towards it. As I drew closer I noticed that its 37-mm. was firing to the north at short intervals, and that its barrel was poked up at an angle of at least 30 degrees. There was no target in sight that I could see; just the big cloud of dust above the invisible escarpment.

From the turret top another Squadron commander was staring through his binoculars, following the high parabola of the shell. He was smoking a pipe. It was the pipe that did it. I told my driver to pull up alongside and as we edged abreast I screamed abuse over the intervening few yards.

"You mucking bastard. You sit there smoking your bloody pipe while my whole squadron's been wiped out. Wiped out, d'you hear? Killed. All of them. See that smoke going up there? Those are Honeys burning. And crews frying. Where are your bloody tanks? Pissing about on the Trigh Capuzzo. Look at that barrel. What are you shooting at—mucking aeroplanes? . . ."

I went on at him while he stared back at me mouth half-open in bewilderment. I heard the sentences ending abruptly as I ran out of breath, and realised suddenly that with the earphones on he could not hear a word. It came to me dimly that later I would be glad that he had not. But I recognised the half-ashamed look on his face as I pulled alongside, and I think he knew that he deserved what I was saying, even if he couldn't hear it. I yelled one final expletive at him and then ordered the driver to advance.

On the way back to battalion H.Q., I asked for the M.O. and an ambulance to be handy for the gunner. As we approached the little cluster of H.Q. tanks a group of officers and N.C.O.s headed by the colonel and Dr. MacMillan walked out to meet me. My driver pulled up about thirty yards from them and I jumped down to run across, the shocked words already bursting on my lips. To my great astonishment I tripped on my first step, and half-fell on to my hands, becoming conscious for the first time of a burning pain in my right foot. I looked down briefly and saw the slit in the toe of my desert boots. But I was too full of other things to think again about it. Surrounded by the H.Q. group I blurted out the hysterical story while the Doc and his orderlies went over to remove the gunner.

The C.O. calmed me with his usual understanding and decency, and then Mac came back and took me off to his truck. He told me the gunner had not been badly wounded . . . flesh wounds in the hand and thigh. He gave me a cup of hot, strong tea, very sweet, and then took off my boot and sock. From my big toe I was startled to see a shining piece of metal protruding, about the size of a marble. He pulled this out with a pair of forceps, washed out the hole and bound it up.

"Now," he said, "Let's have a look at your head."

He went through my hair carefully. Every now and then there would be a little pinging noise and he would locate it with the tweezers and pull out a tiny piece of lead shaving. I could not get rid of my mood. I could not rid my mind of those burning Honeys and the disconsolate survivors and the young officers who would never be able to write home: "Dear Mother, I was in action for the first time today. . . ."

For a few minutes I broke down completely. The doctor,

who knew shock when he saw it, wisely left me alone. Then I washed in a basin of cold water while he poured a jug full of it over my head, and the worst of it was over. I began to think a little more clearly, not of what had just happened but whether there was anything to be done about it. Mac offered to let me spend the night in the comfort of the ambulance, but the thought stayed with me that some of those tank crews might have been able to sneak off into the desert and would be expecting me to do something about them. And there was my own crew to think about.

I limped back to the Honey. It was surrounded by the H.Q. personnel, questioning the driver and operator and inspecting the damage. It was quite an impressive sight. The water cans and outside equipment were a mangled mess. There were six holes in various parts of the armour plating. It looked, and was, a miracle of survival.

While we had been engaged down on the escarpment, the missing squadron that had been away since the Sidi Rezegh battle had rejoined the battalion, and was just about to be sent out with 'A' Squadron on another attack farther along the Trigh Capuzzo. My Honey, though draughty, was still battleworthy, and I was immediately confronted with one of those little moments of decision which can have such far-reaching results. There was no doubt that I could have got out of the battle that evening. If I had done so it was possible that I would not have wanted to come back. I asked the C.O. if there was a spare gunner about the place. He said there was none, but more reinforcements of tanks and men might be coming up that night. I said to my driver and operator, who were just as much concerned in the moment as myself: "Come on then. We'll go without a gunner."

The three of us climbed happily aboard, and I could tell by the looks on their faces that they were glad I had made the decision for them.

Tucked in behind the other squadrons, our Honey moved off west along the Trigh, but my eyes were strained always northwards in the hope of seeing the stray figures that would have been some of my tank crews. Where the ground rose on the right I could see the flashes of German or Italian field-guns and reported them back automatically. Harry Maegraith was hovering protectively near; and with no menace developing, we gained reassurance from the reddening sky and the darkness creeping over the desert behind us. At 5 o'clock we were recalled to H.Q. for replenishment from the lorries which had just arrived and the active day was over.

When night was old enough to obscure our movements, we all moved three miles to the south to what was becoming a familiar leaguer area. There I asked the Colonel's permission to make a patrol at first light to see if I could pick up any of my troops who had managed to get away in the night. He gave a limited approval—I was not to go beyond the Trigh Capuzzo and I was not on any account to get out of wireless touch. It was a case of yesterday is past; there is still to-morrow.

Before I rolled up in my blankets Mac came along to give me a good slug of brandy and two pills to produce the oblivion I needed.

That night, a few miles away across the desert, an officer of the German Artillery Regiment 33 was writing in the regimental War Diary:

"A group of enemy tanks attacked the supply vehicles in the rear of the division. They burst right into the middle of the column and fired shells and machine-gun bullets into the vehicles, which were pushing forward at full speed. Batterien 6 and 8 immediately swung their guns round, but the dust was so thick they could see nothing until suddenly an enemy tank appeared in a cloud of dust about 50 metres in front of

the gun positions of Batterie 6. We immediately opened up
over open sights. The tank burst into flames. Another tank
just behind it was knocked out. In a very short time the Batterie destroyed 10 more enemy tanks at point blank range,
and thus beat off the attack on the division's rear."

Eleventh Day

IN the night they took away my battered tank. By the time I had been shaken into wakefulness at first light. Maegraith had reorganised my own crew and the rest of the squadron with the reinforcements that had come up with the rations and petrol. 'C' Squadron was now five tanks strong, including mine and Maegraith's. I had a quick word with the new crews, a few of whom were from the battalion's regular reserve pool, and then Harry and I set off towards the Trigh Capuzzo.

The top of the sky was bright, but the earth stayed as sombre as my mood as we reached the edge of the nearest escarpment. I was not at all sure of my position in relation to the previous afternoon's events, but from the crest of the ridge we commanded a wide view to the north. The desert lay silent and empty before us as we probed the scrub and rock with the binoculars, eager for the little movement or the patch of khaki that would reveal a man. It stared back at us blankly.

Directly below us the highway of tracks stretched dark and deserted, linking the horizons. Up and down the crest we ran, hoping that by noise and movement we would attract the attention of any stray troopers skulking in the fear of uncertainty. The noise of the radial engines was as distinct from the rumbling beat of the Diesels as a xylophone from a double bass. The encroaching light lit up all the plateau, but gave us no glimpse of the aftermath of yesterday's battle, and I realised that we must be several miles west of where we had begun our descent to disaster. The C.O.'s voice interrupted my contemplation of the next decision, recalling us urgently to H.Q.

On the run back we were attracted by a little cluster of Honeys encircling several mounds thrown up from a group of slit trenches. Full of curiosity we trundled over, and I recognised the tanks as belonging to 5 Royal Tank Regiment. From their hesitancy I thought there must be at least one concealed anti-tank gun and a mine-field in those mounds, but as I drove up alongside the slit trenches all I found in the bottom of each one was a terrified German infantryman. I beckoned to them to come out, which they did with white faces, upraised arms and very obvious relief. I passed them over to the 5th Tanks, made a rude gesture with my fingers at the troop commander and carried on back to the battalion.

Back at H.Q. we learnt that a column of lorried infantry was reported to be forming up four miles to the north-west. We had been ordered to attack it. I swanned off with my five-tank squadron, shedding my depression in the contemplation of renewed action, obliterating the past once again by over-crowding the present. My troop had just crossed the Trigh when we ran slap into a number of scattered enemy vehicles and troops that seemed to appear from nowhere without very much idea of anywhere to go.

Immediately the Honeys came under fire from several anti-tank guns mounted on the backs of trucks. At the same moment the C.O. came on the air to tell us to move fast on a completely different bearing westwards to give assistance to 22nd Armoured Brigade, who were engaging M.E.T. and tanks. I could not disengage from the brisk little battle that had developed all round us. Once you are entangled with anti-tank guns you have to go on with everything you've got until one or the other is eliminated. All five of my tanks were blazing away with their Brownings; within a minute or two

the Jerries had had enough, and were pulling out with ourselves in full pursuit.

I had a hectic chase after one truck which was bouncing
all over the uneven surface as it fled, with the men on the
back swaying wildly and firing their gun desperately every
few seconds. My own machine-gun fire seemed to be equally
inaccurate, and finally I told the driver to halt and the gunner
to fire the cannon. We were only 50 yards away; and as I
did not see the shot strike, it must have been the noise that
frightened the truck driver into a swerving halt. The occupants jumped down on to the sand in surrender.

Suddenly the whole desert seemed to be swarming with
little groups of Germans anxious to give themselves up. The
other Honeys clattered around like broody hens collecting
little coveys of the Afrika Korps. Soon the armour-plating
of the tanks was completely camouflaged by the dark figures
of men. It presented me with a pretty little problem. I had
been given my orders, but by this time the rest of the battalion
was out of sight and I had only the vaguest idea where it was.
I could not contact the Colonel on the set, and I could hardly
go charging into a tank v. tank battle with the Honeys
festooned with Germans. I decided to try to locate Brigade
headquarters, off-load the prisoners and get a proper bearing
to where the battle was being fought.

After a few minutes' run we picked out the package of
tanks and vehicles denoting Brigade some miles to the south.
When we halted just outside the area I made all the prisoners
line up in a double column. The Brigadier himself came over
to see me looking, I thought, very cross. He glanced casually
at the prisoners and then asked me what the hell I thought I
was doing swanning round the desert picking up bodies when
I should be with the battalion fighting tanks.

I was half-expecting a raspberry, but it was hardly fair in
the circumstances. I pointed out that most of the prisoners

were anti-tank gunners, that we had knocked out four anti-tank guns, and I did not like the idea of leaving all those men free to knock us out the next day or the day after that.

"Who knows?" I said. "One of these chaps here may have knocked out your own tank by this time tomorrow."

I think he saw my point, and when I asked him for my battalion position he told me that the situation was a bit confused and that I'd better stick around until he knew more of what was happening. Somebody came rushing over to tell Gatehouse that he could see a number of enemy tanks approaching from the north. Glad of the interruption and of the opportunity of getting away from there I collected my five Honeys and we left in a hurry.

A dozen tanks of various sizes were moving slowly along the Trigh in a small packet from the west. I guessed that they had been sent back to see what had happened to the group we had run into earlier. There was no chance of finding any cover. The desert between us was as flat as a salt-pan. As soon as they saw the Honeys they adopted their usual tactics of sending out a screen of light tanks, and about half a dozen Mark IIs came swarming out to meet us. There was nothing we could do about it except stay where we were, waiting for the right range to take a crack at them. This lack of reaction seemed to disconcert the German tank commanders, for they slowed down in uncertainty and then came to an irresolute halt.

I wasn't looking for a battle on terms of two to one, including a number of Mark IIIs and IVs, so we just sat there hoping that they would sheer off and leave Brigade alone. Then the light tanks must have got some pretty blistering instructions, for they suddenly came forward again, though a good deal more cautiously, and with their guns puffing ineffectual smoke at us.

The Honeys stayed silent until the Jerries were about 900

yards away; then I said into the mike "O.K. Get cracking." The 37-mms blazed into action, and within a few seconds I was overjoyed to see two panzers come to a stop and the crews bale out. Then the shelling started from the bigger tanks in the rear. For the time being we ignored this as we kept moving slightly to and fro across the front of the light tanks, who had pressed on to about 600 yards and then decided they had had enough. From one of these a slow wreath of smoke drifted, and I saw the driver leap out of the front, but no turret opened.

Then the big panzers came crunching towards us, and the shell fire from the Mark IVs' big guns was being aimed directly at our Honeys. I wasn't going to wait until we came within range of the 50-mm. armour-piercing shell of the Mark IIIs, and I ordered the troop commanders to pull back slowly. They knew the form. The drivers went into reverse, and we backed away, firing all the time.

100 yards on my left I saw a Honey come to a stop with one of its tracks dangling shattered and useless over the front sprocket. Three of the crew spilled out of the turret and crouched down behind the engine. I waved to them to run over, and then concentrated again on the approaching panzers. When I looked again the disabled Honey was a good 200 yards away, and the crew had not moved from its protection. One of them waved to me and again I signalled to them to make a run for it. I thought briefly of the brigade order about picking up crews. I couldn't risk the tank, and I was supposed to set an example. I couldn't understand why they just sat there, unwilling to risk the bullets and shells in the face of certain capture.

Things were getting pretty hot for the remaining Honeys, and I knew that my own tank had been hit several times. I did not quite know what to do if the panzers kept on coming forward. I looked over my shoulder and saw the Brigade H.Q.

vehicles clustered where we had left them, a couple of miles away but already coming within range of the Mark IVs. All we could do, I decided, was to carry on as we were in the hope that something would happen that was outside our own control.

We moved slowly back, red tracers streaking towards the enemy, aware of the death cleaving the air about us. The panzers moved forward, conforming to our withdrawal but not pressing us, apparently just as lacking in enthusiasm as we were. Soon their intentions became clear. The big tanks were concerned with recovering their own casualties and the crew of the Honey, and had no offensive design beyond that. Through binoculars I saw the dispirited troopers slouch over to a big Mark IV and clamber on to the back. For a minute or two everything stayed motionless then the panzers started pulling back in twos and threes, leaving a watchful screen behind them. The last few light tanks darted back . . . the battle was over.

We went back, just the four of us, to Brigade where Gatehouse and some of his staff officers had been watching the whole performance through their binoculars. I had a quick look round the outside of the Honey and then, still smarting a little over the morning's rebuke, went over to the brigadier's group. Full of righteousness, I said: "I reckon we've just saved your headquarters from being over-run."

Gatehouse said: "You were fighting at pretty long range, weren't you?"

"If you think that was long range, sir, go and have a look at my tank."

I took them over to the Honeys and led them round, pointing out the holes in the armour-plating, in the toolboxes, in the bedding rolls, and the 30-mm. shell embedded in the front plate.

"Six bloody holes in my tank . . . even at long range."

There was no further comment, and when I asked for a bearing back to the battalion Alec Gatehouse, friendly again, told me that he had ordered 3rd and 5th Tanks to rally back, and that they would be coming in soon.

Doc MacMillan was at Brigade H.Q., which formed a rendezvous when a battle was on for all those not actively engaged in the fighting. He came over with Harry Maegraith, after attending to one of our wounded. Doc said : "Well done, Bob. Last night I told the C.O. I thought it would be a good idea if you had a short rest. I was wrong."

I knew what he meant, and how much it meant. He appreciated the little personal crisis I had survived. Now that it was over it was as though a curtain had been drawn across a corner of my mind. Yesterday, with all its horror and shock, had disappeared in the past.

The rest of the battalion, minus three more Honeys lost in the morning's encounter, came back about noon. 8th Hussars were still out keeping an eye on the enemy forces now reported to be withdrawing north-west. During the lunch break the Colonel came round to pass on a message the brigadier had received from the new commander-in-chief. It congratulated the brigade on its splendid work, and promised that after the next task we would be rested.

In the light of events this was a rather extraordinary message. The previous night Ritchie had sent a message to 30 Corps urging that "it was of the utmost importance to prevent the enemy escaping westward, south of the Sidi Rezegh escarpment". The enemy, in fact, was not dreaming of escaping westward or in any other direction. He was concentrating his armoured divisions for the annihilation of the New Zealanders at Sidi Rezegh before they could link up with the Tobruk garrison. What we had failed to do the previous day and this day was prevent the junction of the two panzer divisions moving west from the frontier, with Ariete Division moving north from El Gubi.

We had failed not because we had suffered military defeat in the battle, but because of the routine procedure of retiring from the scene of operations each night to a comparatively secluded leaguer. The enemy had taken full advantage of this gratuitous freedom, and by the time the British army commanders realised Rommel's intentions the concentration of his armour had been virtually completed and he was able to repulse our tank attacks while gathering his strength for the assault on the New Zealanders.

However, none of these events and intentions were apparent to the tank crews as we absorbed the warm glow of the C.-in-C.'s message. Obviously, they were not very apparent to anybody else either.

After lunch the whole of 4th Armoured moved leisurely off to the north-west, where it was to cover the right flank of the South Africans on their way up to Sidi Rezegh. An hour later we were in distant contact with a large enemy force of tanks and M.E.T. which, for some reason, we were content to shell at long-range inducing some mild retaliation. There seemed to be a universal unwillingness at that moment to start something we couldn't finish. In the night we marched interminably back to the leaguer area—due south into the open desert.

Twelfth and Thirteenth Days

THE 'B' echelon party with our petrol, rations and ammunition failed to arrive during the night, and we had barely enough fuel to disperse at first light. It always alarmed me to think what might happen if we were caught by some stray panzer column, immobile and without ammunition for our guns. The enemy, it later transpired, was probably a good deal worse off than we were in the matter of supplies, and the war diaries of the Afrika Korps are full of references to the shortage of fuel and shells. Certainly we missed a number of glorious opportunities of inflicting damage on the enemy when he was thus handicapped—chiefly through lack of experience and the proper equipment, mental as well as material.

A patrol was sent out to find the replenishment party, and we lay around in open formation, glad of the chance to make a quick brew in spite of the shortage of petrol. The officers congregated around the C.O.'s tank in the perpetual quest for the real gen. On this morning the total tank strength of the battalion was 14, half of 'A' Squadron having gone astray somewhere the previous evening. Proper organisation was impossible, and 'C' Squadron was reduced to myself, Harry Maegraith, a sergeant and a corporal, with 4 Honeys.

It was obvious that as a battalion we could no longer undertake anything very significant unless reinforced, and the rest of the brigade was in very similar plight. This was appreciated in the continuing rôle of protection to the South Africans.

Things did not seem to be going too well with them. I overheard a staff officer saying to our C.O.: "Uncle George is all right, and Uncle George's boys are all right; but Uncle George's nephew is just bloody awkward. We can't get him to fight a battle, or even to move to a place where he might have to fight a battle."

After the mauling and virtual elimination of 5th S.A. Brigade at Sidi Rezegh, there was a natural reluctance to incur heavy casualties in the remaining force. It must be remembered that those Commonwealth divisions represented an extremely high proportion of the country's most valuable manpower. Very often this reluctance to incur casualties was inspired from above and not by internal and local influences. Perhaps it is as well to leave what, at the time, was a contentious subject with the comment that Dan Pienaar may have overdone the interpretation of suggestions made to him not to risk any more disasters.

It was this need for affording protection to the South Africans, combined perhaps with the intention to give us a bit of a break, that resulted in 4th Armoured being uncommitted to any decisive action for a considerable time. It was all the more strange because the campaign was entering a curious phase in which a major effort by Eighth Army, with a concentration of all its available tank strength, could have forced a decision in one all-out, conclusive battle south-east of Tobruk. Instead, the struggle went on piece-meal all over the desert, with Rommel fending off disjointed attacks while he planned the crucial moment and what he hoped would be the crucial blow. It was at this critical time that the Army commander sent a signal to Gatehouse that his task for the day was to keep open the road to the New Zealanders, to follow the South African brigade on its move towards the airfield and "keep a look-out".

Accordingly we spent a very peaceful morning looking-out and seeing nothing except the slow, spasmodic movement of the groups of South African transport along the skyline to the west. Over the northern horizon there was much heavy gun-fire interjected with the heavier crumph of bombs.

It was the first time we had become visually aware of the intensity of the air activity and of the R.A.F.'s superiority. The planes, mostly Boston bombers, came over in tight-knit packets, black against the overhang or faint and almost transparent against the blue. When they were little dots in the north they would suddenly be surrounded by dissolving satellites of ack-ack fire, and would wheel away to the right, always keeping the same unbroken formation. Slowly above the desert the tops of dirty explosions would lift, and we would hear the thud of bombs.

We dozed in the turrets or chewed ruminantly on biscuit and marmalade until late in the morning, when the crackles in the earphones gave way to the information that enemy tanks were massing to attack "friends on Sidi Rezegh" and we were to stand by to go to their assistance. All the brigade's field-guns, covered by a squadron of tanks from 5R.T.R., were sent off. We were glad it wasn't us. Boredom had become a precious thing.

By 2 o'clock the brigade was on the move northward. Within an hour we were passing through a grim-looking concentration of burnt-out vehicles, abandoned and wrecked guns and tanks, and the quick mounds of new-filled graves for which the numerous slit-trenches provided such a ready catacomb. Suddenly I recognized it as the area in which we had fought on Totensonntag—a dim nightmare of a memory, not seven days old.

3R.T.R. formed the protection on the right during this move. All the activity was on the left, thank goodness, where other elements of the brigade were in constant and violent contiguity with the Italian armour still moving up from Bir el Gubi to join the panzers.

It was the sort of fluid situation, in which, with infantry positions menaced by enemy tanks, all sorts of threats and possibilities of annihilation were liable to develop in the trench-bound mind. In that sort of situation there is very little difference between reality and imagination, and nobody ever waits to make quite sure.

Between 3 o'clock and 6 o'clock our Honeys rushed in quick succession southwards, northwards and westwards. The only reason we did not rush eastwards was that, so far as we knew, there was no British infantry in that direction for 60 miles. During these hectic alarums and excursions to rescue over-run riflemen and gunners my Honey did not fire a single shot, nor did I see a single thing to shoot at except a curious flight of strange birds that I have never seen before or since. They came wheeling over the desert, in a very tight formation, about 20 of them, the size of pigeons but slimmer and hard-looking, and settled on a cluster of rocks about 40 yards in front of the tank. They immediately went into a stiff pose in unison, each bird acting independently but with joint design to form a picture of an outcrop of shaley rock. They had long beaks which they pointed stiffly at an angle of 45 degrees. They were surrounded by noise and movement of a sort which they could never have dreamt of, yet they never flickered an eyelid or twitched a single, rigid, grey-black feather. I was completely absorbed in this dedicated immobility and ran my Honey up to within 10 yards of them. Only at that distance did they lose their corporate pattern and become individual birds. I fired a shot from my .38 revolver into the ground beside them. They literally never blinked an eyelid. I climbed down from the turret and walked to within three yards of them. They stayed fixed in their rock-like trance. I edged forward gently until I was right above them. Twenty eyes looked at me intelligently and I began to get a queer feeling that in a few minutes I would turn into something lithic myself and spend the rest of my days out-staring those birds.

It was quite an effort to bend forward and stretch out my hand. Twenty eyes swivelled silently and simultaneously in those entranced bodies, following the movement. When my hand was about four inches from the nearest bird all of them, activated by a single purpose and single mind, suddenly took flight—many-winged but cohesive—and disappeared away to the east. I stared unbelievingly at the barren ground where they had been rooted. A fairly adjacent shell-burst restored me noisily to reality, and I hurried back into the turret.

That night we moved back to leaguer in a march that I thought was never going to end. With the blackness of night engulfing us and the sand and dust pouring into our confined, hard world, we turned our backs on the bright lights of the German positions and clanked chain-like into the empty south. The wireless sets in each Honey were tuned in to stations all over Europe and the Middle East, anywhere there was music, to keep driver and commander awake. One tank deviating from the line of march would take half the battalion blundering off sleepily into the night. It was an extra and alarming responsibility for tank commanders and drivers who had been without anything more than a few snatched hours of sleep each night for two weeks—and that, moreover, at the end of days full of nerve-racking fear and hideous activity or, at the least, hours and hours of eye-straining vigil.

Not until three hours and ten miles later were we arranged in our phalanxed, armoured dormitories, dropping down on hard-found bits of soft sand among the pebbles and rocks. At midnight a D.R. came round, breaking through the blankets of unconsciousness, to summon squadron commanders to a conference at the Colonel's tank.

"Christ Almighty," I muttered as I stumbled dazedly away from sleep "Why couldn't they just let me stay a lieutenant?"

The C.O. greeted us wearily, and as we clustered round the inevitable map, he told us that all the armour that was left in 30 Corps was to be concentrated under Gatehouse. This meant that the surviving Crusader tanks of 22nd Armoured Brigade were to be handed over. There were only 25 of them left, but with reinforcements that were arriving that night, the total strength of the 4th Armoured would be brought up to 120 tanks—more than we had had for many days, but still well short of the full complement.

On hearing this, most of us thought it could only be a prelude to some new violence and an ending of the period of inconclusiveness of the past few days. We were surprised and, I believe, genuinely disappointed that instead of a decisive encounter battle with the panzer divisions which would end up in us either being buried in the sand or else taken on an heroic return to Cairo, we were to continue our rôle of protection and to harass and destroy the enemy as opportunity offered.

This sort of vague instruction usually results in nothing happening at all. The thirteenth day was no exception. It was an almost exact replica of the previous day, with all its alarums and especially its excursions. All day long, too, we heard the gunfire in the north and wondered what it was all about and who was winning. Nobody told us.

Back again in leaguer at night we were greatly pleased to hear that 5th Tanks had had a considerable set-to with Ariete Division away on our left flank, and that Paddy Doyle's squadron of Honeys had knocked out sixteen M13s. We all wanted to have a crack at the Eyeties, and I could never understand why we were not launched in a full-scale attack on Ariete. There were plenty of opportunities after they had left the minefields of El Gubi.

Fourteenth Day

THE second crisis had come swiftly at Sidi Rezegh. Failure to relieve the pressure on the New Zealand Division (it was our failure, but not our fault) had put them in an impossible position, and made our inactivity of the past two days plainly culpable.

Long before sunrise we were wakened by urgent orders to move at all speed to the airfield to assist the withdrawal of the New Zealanders, who were in grave danger of being over-run. It was a shock to us to discover that our complete ignorance of the course the battle was taking, except in our limited vicinity, was concealing a set-back of such magnitude.

Before the sun had risen the whole brigade was on the move to Sidi Rezegh, that fateful and fatal magnet whose significance still seemed to elude the comprehension of the higher command. Our 3rd Battalion travelled on the right flank, furthest away from the enemy. The brigade centre-line was directed straight at the airfield, and we sped north, each Honey a rosy blob in the sunrise, the dew-soaked sand yielding no dust. As the desert lit up it revealed familiar birs and cairns that we had been passing and repassing, repeating and repeating in our wireless chatter, every day since the campaign opened. The sombre relics of earlier battles surrounded us, as familiar and static as the cairns and contours.

Looking over towards the clouds of dust and unsightly smoke that seemed to hang permanently between the escarpments of Sidi Rezegh, I wondered if the air above that contested strip of earth would ever be clear again.

With the daylight and increasing visibility came the shells, scattering broadly among us as we rumbled forward. My troop was up in protection front—it had become an automatic rôle —and I could hear the quick whine and bang of the missiles as they passed close overhead seeking the bigger concentrations behind.

Through the murk of morning enemy guns flashed along the distant crests. There was no need to report their position; half-a-dozen O.P.s would already have spotted them and be plotting their position for counter-battery fire. Soon, and once again, my three Honeys were poised on the edge of the scarp. It was almost the identical spot where, just eight days of a lifetime before, I had gaped at the fantastic scene below while the long brigadier had hammered on the walls of my tank.

I half-expected to see him again, dashing up to me in his little car with the blond hair of his driver gleaming in the sunlight. For down in that embattled depression and stretching away to the north over the next drop was just such another scene of angry chaos.

The landing ground was still a mass of disintegrated vehicles, and the same planes stood around the edges, blackened and forlorn. But now vehicles were moving away in a steady stream over the flank of the depression where the land takes another step down to the sea. In the midst of it all the tomb of Saint Rezegh gleamed white and unforgettable.

What astonished me most was that the ridge opposite me, and all of the feature known as Point 175, seemed to be in the occupation of the enemy. I could see them quite clearly through my binoculars about three miles away—men and trucks and unmistakable Italian tanks. And they were in the rear of the New Zealanders. Once again, it was a tactical situation which was beyond my capacity to envisage, but which just had to be accepted since it was there—along with all the other unexpected and apparently impossible situations which had confronted us throughout the campaign and which were dealt with or avoided on the spur of the moment.

It was 7.30 in the morning when my troop arrived at the southernmost escarpment. The next few hours have been variously recorded in half a dozen regimental diaries and histories. My own recollections of the events of that morning do not seem to bear very much resemblance to any of the official versions. It is not easy for me to think that it all happened in my imagination; I was there at the time.

By 8 o'clock we had orders to push on to contact the New Zealanders and ensure their safe withdrawal from the enemy. Accordingly, we set off down the long slope coming under heavy fire from the right all the way. This petered out as we got beyond vision. By-passing the airfield on our left, my troop was very soon perched on the second escarpment directly above the Trigh Capuzzo. Shells of all calibres were churning up the earth in and around a dispersed group of vehicles left behind to transport the New Zealand rearguard.

I asked the C.O. for further instructions, and was ordered to contact the New Zealand commander (if I could find him) and tell him that he was to withdraw immediately through our tanks. We pushed on down across the road and pulled up behind a cluster of derelict vehicles, including one Matilda I-tank. There I got down and walked forward to where I could have a good look at the ground ahead. I was unwilling to take my Honey out on to open ground most of which, if our information was true, was already in the hands of the enemy. I felt singularly exposed, but the thought of being hit by a stray piece of shrapnel worried me less than being obliterated by a direct hit from an 88. Harry Maegraith joined me, and we peered through our binoculars from behind the thick comfort of the Matilda. About 100 yards in front I saw within the converging O of my glasses an officer sitting with his back to me on the edge of a slit trench, his feet dangling inside.

"Christmas night, Harry; isn't that Freyberg sitting there?"

"It certainly looks like the pictures of him. What the hell's he doing there?"

"Well, whoever it is," I said, "he's the chap to give the message to."

"Shall I go, Bob?"

"No. You wait here. If it is Freyberg, it's a man I've always wanted to meet."

"If you can find anybody to introduce you . . ." Harry was saying when we were astonished to see a solitary German lorry coming along the Trigh from the west. It drove right past the remnants of the New Zealanders, right past my troop, and headed straight for battalion headquarters behind me. Alongside the lorry galloped a little black and white dog, like a fox terrier. We watched it, grinning, imagining the consternation on the driver's face when he found himself in the middle of a lot of British tanks.

Just to make sure I sent Harry running back to his Honey to tell the C.O. what was coming towards him. You never know with these things: it may have had Rommel in the front. Just then the driver realised his mistake, whirled the vehicle round in a great cloud of spurting sand, and tore back along the road. Behind it the fox terrier was stretched out like a greyhound, yapping like mad. I heard a few Brownings barking in pursuit, but the lorry and the dog got clean away. We didn't mind particularly.

After this diversion I left the shelter of the I-tank and walked forward, a little tremulously but sustained by that nonchalant figure by the slit trench. I covered the 100 yards as casually as I could, struggling not to throw myself flat on my face every time I heard the whine and crunch of a shell. I halted behind a broad back and said "Sir!" loudly above the enveloping noise.

The officer's rank was concealed from me under some sort of jerkin but there was no mistaking that face. I saluted smartly as he looked round.

"Third Tank Battalion, Fourth Armoured Brigade, sir. I have a message for the commanding officer, New Zealand Division."

"Then you'd better give it to me, my boy. And get into this slit trench while you're at it."

"I can give it to you standing, thank you sir. It's not a long message . . . thank God."

He grinned up at me and I told him that he was to pull out eastwards right away, that our Honeys were in position to cover his withdrawal. I pointed them out to him, where they stood patient in that derelict litter.

"Right. I hope the car is a runner." He indicated a big Humber staff car nearby. I heard a new sound now, the quick zip and chatter of machine-gun bullets. I saluted again and beat it.

Back behind the jilted fortress of the Matilda, Maegraith and I watched Freyberg as he summoned the last of his officers and men. Twelve or fifteen soldiers got up out of the scrub and sand, and clambered into and all over the staff car. There was the usual moment of doubt and then, with men festooned all over the bonnet, mudguards and boot, it wheeled about, sped past us and vanished down the Trigh Capuzzo. I felt a nudge from Harry.

Coming down the slope into the area that had just been occupied by the New Zealanders was a long column of dark-coated men, four abreast, that seemed to stretch back indefinitely. We could not see the end of it over the next escarpment. They threaded their way slowly, disinterestedly, through the abandoned transport, slit trenches and shell-holes.

They were not more than 500 yards away from us, and I looked at them, almost unbelieving, through my glasses. I have never seen such a jaded, dispirited lot of men.

Many of them were capless, and the slanting rays of the early sun revealed starkly the dirt and dishevellment, the weariness of the spirit reflected in those weary faces. They shuffled glumly down the slope, eyes on the ground immediately about them, not once looking up towards our tanks or the departing New Zealand troops. They came to a shambling sort of halt, looking about for a place where they could conveniently go to ground.

Maegraith and I raced for our tanks. I got on the air to the C.O. and told him of the wonderful target that was waiting just ahead adding that we were about to engage with machine-gun fire. His reply was a trifle disturbing:

"Never mind about that just now. We've been surrounded. We're to fight our way out and try to rally three miles south of the airfield. Move at once."

I scanned the empty crests and depressions to the south, and the gloomy column of enemy still standing in doleful ranks. I looked across at Harry. He lifted his hands shoulder high in the turret in an expressive, despairing gesture and we followed on behind the wheeling Honeys of the rest of the battalion. I kept my binoculars on the German infantry. As far as I could see they displayed no interest whatever in our presence or our movement. One thing was clear—if the enemy had just won another Sidi Rezegh battle, those blokes didn't know it.

Every minute as we sped back towards the rallying point I expected to hear the earphones burst into life with the first frantic reports of enemy tanks. Nothing happened, and we climbed out on to that familiar plateau above the landing ground like friendly dogs returning to the well-savoured odours of an accustomed lamp-post after an inter-suburban frolic.

Long after, this incident was graphically recalled, and confirmed, for me by the account of the official New Zealand war historian who was wounded and captured in that vicinity at the time. He was in a forward dressing station which had been overrun by the German attack on the previous evening, and was a witness of much of the morning's activity. This is what he wrote: "My firm impression, and also General Kippenberger's, was that the German troops who passed through or near the M.D.S. at that time were practically sleepwalkers and certainly did not regard themselves as victorious. I think their morale was very near breaking point . . .".

Back at the rallying point, reached without sight let alone sound of the enemy, we were remote enough from danger to meet our replenishment vehicles and top up with petrol. We hadn't used any ammo.

For the rest of the afternoon we watched aeroplanes. It was exciting to see the nervous coveys of Stukas making their quick, frightened raids and breaking up in terror as the Spitfires and Hurricanes pounced. After our experience in Greece, dominated by the German dive-bombers, there was no more pleasant or rewarding sight than to watch the Stukas wheeling and twisting and side-slipping clumsily in front of the fighters. The swoop of the Spitfire would be followed by a black surge of smoke from the Stuka, and then the wild, vertical plunge and crash into eternity.

In the evening, when the sky grew red and the desert grew dark, fighter patrols and the swift couples of photo-reconnaissance planes flew casually back across the battlefield. We watched them enviously. In an hour's time, bathed, shaved and feeling the cleanness of clean clothes, their pilots would be yelling for taxis heading for the Dug-out under the Hotel

Metropole or the roof-garden on top of the Continental, listening to that ripe plum of a female singing "Sand in my Shoes".
There would be iced lager at Tommy's bar, martinis on the
verandah at Shepheard's, while the girl friends were rounded
up for the dinner-dance at Gezira. Soft lights, soft music,
bright tablecloths, a flask of wine and thou ... What was that
lovely American girl doing now? ...

So the planes winged back through an afternoon sky, over
a land where it was already night; the long escarpment of Sidi
Rezegh stretched across the horizon full of Germans and
Italians.

'God in heaven,' I thought, 'it was like this before we
started. Is nobody ever going to win this bloody war?'

In the darkness we moved back to deep-rutted Bir Berraneb.

Fifteenth and Sixteenth Days

THE next few days stay with me as a confusion of movement in which we moved everywhere and never got
anywhere. It was a period in which we seemed to be
disembodied from the main battle—the struggle for decision
going on always beyond the next crest. Hour became indis-
tinguishable from hour, surrounded by a monotony of same-
ness in the confined desert round which we moved like bulky
and uneconomical errand boys. Somehow the high tempo of
the battle had vanished, and with it the crusading spirit that
had inspired us in that bright beginning. We were all, I think,
past the climax of endeavour, approaching a point of mental
and physical exhaustion. Subconsciously we realised that the
crisis of this battle was over and that the victory, though invisible, was present there in the dust and days and death
ahead. For us it coincided with a moment, undefinable in time,
when there is a realisation that the future is real again and
important and that you yourself want to be in it. It is not a
good way for the fighting man to feel. It happens to them all
—some a good deal sooner than others. The New Zealand
General Kippenberger relates a curious story to show that
such feelings are pretty universal . . .

At the end of that first day of December, as the victorious
enemy forces re-occupied the vital spaces around Sidi Rezegh,
a German artillery officer limped up to him in the captured
dressing station in which he had been made prisoner, and
said: "We have retaken Belhamed and our eastern and

western forces have joined hands. But it is no use. We have lost the battle. Our losses are too heavy. We have lost the battle."

That German officer was past the zenith. He had reached the point where the future was more important than the present.

The trial of strength had taken place. The issue had been decided, no matter how many battles were still to be fought and how many graves were still to be scratched in the sand. There was nothing conclusive in the dispositions of either side. There was still an apparent stalemate and on the face of it the Axis armies had won an important victory. But on our side we all felt that although we had practically no idea of what was going on, we were not going to end up on the losing side. We couldn't put it any stronger than that.

For two days we lay at Bir Berraneb. There was plenty to do . . . maintenance of tanks and guns, laundering of clothes and hair, laborious shaving, reorganisation of the battalion with the arrival of reinforcements and the loan of a squadron from 8th Hussars. The tank strength of 3R.T.R. was now about 40, and a good deal of rearranging was made even more necessary by the posting to 'B' echelon of the 'A' squadron commander. I was sorry for the major, a regular officer, whose foolishness would set him back many years on the overcrowded ladder of seniority.

I became second-in-command of 'C' squadron once more under "Withers", an efficient regular sergeant-major before the war, who had gone through O.C.T.U. in the Westminster Dragoons at the same time as I had. I wasn't in the least bit upset. I knew it had to happen as soon as we were brought up to strength. All I wanted was the war to finish as quickly as possible so that I could get to hell out of it. And I was still left

more or less to my own resources with my troop; neither did
I have to deal with all the administrative bumf.

During this rest period we were told the army commander's
plans for the immediate future. This was to clean up the
area north of El Gubi with the Indian Brigade, assisted by I-
tanks. This would isolate that strongly defended position due
south of El Adem and Tobruk, and by further penetration
westwards it was hoped to make both Gubi and Tobruk un-
tenable. The ultimate object stayed the same—destruction of
the German-Italian forces to prevent their regrouping back
in Tripolitania to start the whole deadly, weary business all
over again. Possession of the ground without the destruction
of the enemy was, in the desert, quite purposeless—as a whole
stream of commanders on both sides discovered between 1939
and 1943.

The rôle of destruction in this case had been allotted to
4th Armoured Brigade. I had the impression that we were
going about it in a rather curious way, but I am sure this had
very little to do with Gatehouse's wishes and I was beginning
to appreciate that the simple issues of a local situation in war
become vastly more complicated in the aggregate back at
Army headquarters. I could never get rid of the thought,
though, that if all the simple issues were resolved simply
then the final pattern would lose a great deal of its com-
plexity.

Our immediate purpose in this phase of the Crusader
campaign was to prevent armoured interference with the
infantry attack on El Gubi, and prevent any enemy forces
withdrawing northwards as a result of the attack. In the early
morning, therefore, the whole brigade positioned itself in
the area between El Gubi and El Adem, where we sat more or
less motionless all the morning and the greater part of the
afternoon. 'C' squadron was on the extreme northern flank

of this immobile manœuvre. Becoming bored and eye-sore
with too much watching, I went off alone on a little jaunt to
the first of the big escarpments to the north.

There was usually some activity going on up there, and
you could see something coming long before they could see
you. Sure enough, when I reached that long ridge that seemed
to stretch the whole length of the North African littoral I
became immediately aware of the vast movement of vehicles
and tanks *eastward* through the Sidi Rezegh depression and
away along the familiar highway of the Trigh Capuzzo. Such
a large-scale movement in that direction did not fit in anywhere with the tactical situation that had been described to
us the previous evening.

I went as close as I dared to establish positively that it was
a German column, and then got on the air to the C.O., in a
state of considerable excitement. I thought it was the beginning of another Rommel dash to The Wire and our rear areas.
The Colonel told me to keep out of the way and watch developments, and he would contact me again after he had
been in touch with Brigade. So I sat and watched the long,
dust-covered convoy, the grim panzers sliding along the flanks
like destroyers round a fleet of merchant ships. The C.O. came
back on the blower to tell me that Army knew all about the
move, that Rommel was apparently trying to relieve his forces
bottled-up in Bardia and Sollum, and that it was being taken
care of. In the meantime I was to keep an eye on them, but
not to get committed.

"None of your bloody nonsense, Bob," he said. "We'll need
every tank we've got for the next operation."

I was a bit exposed perched on that rim of rock, so I sneaked
along to a place where the ground was broken by low sand
ridges which enabled me to get up to within 500 yards of the
column of M.E.T. as they moved slowly on. I kept on thinking

of Bardia, where they were heading; Bardia with its lighthouse that I had looked down upon that second afternoon. Now, more than two weeks later, the enemy was still in Bardia and here was the whole Afrika Korps, 500 yards away, heading towards it along the Trigh Capuzzo.

How many times had I crossed the Trigh since the first elated day? But it was still an Axis highway, and Bardia was still an Axis fort.

Crouched behind a convenient hummock I reckoned we were secure enough in that light to have a brew. There had been no other opportunity that day, and we could never make one in leaguer with its strict orders against lights. I sent the gunner and operator out to make the tea while I kept wireless watch. The driver stayed at his controls, with engine ticking over, just in case.

The packed rows of lorries passing along before me were an inviting machine-gun target, and I could picture the flap that would result from a couple of quick bursts. I did not want to do anything that would interrupt our tea-party, but could not help thinking that if Army were really taking care of this enemy move they would be plastering it with everything they had got.

The glow of sunset was turning to the purple prelude of night before the end of that column passed across my front. I was sitting on top of the turret sipping tea when suddenly two squat, sinister shapes detached themselves from the rearmost group of panzers and came swiftly out straight for me. I yelled at the gunner and operator, lolling in the sand over their steaming mugs, and they clambered past me down into the turret, not however letting go of their tea. I told Whaley to start reversing slowly so that we would not attract too much attention but could get away from the dwindling smoke from our fire. I think it was that which had attracted the panzers, and not the Honey. I doubted whether they could even see it. We had gone about 30 yards backwards when the engine spluttered to a stop to be followed by a now familiar noise— the ineffectual whirring of the self-starter.

"O.K., Whaley, don't tell me. We're out of petrol," I said into the mike. "Better load both guns. But I don't think we're going to need them."

The two panzers had come to a halt about 400 yards away. I could only just see them in the gloom, and I was pretty sure they could barely see me. Certainly they could not know that I was out there all on my own. After a few minutes of steadily watching each other I think both sides accepted that nothing aggressive was contemplated, and my mind turned to the next problem—how to get out of there.

I switched the set to 'send': "Hullo, MABO, MABO One calling. I have run out of petrol at map reference figures . . . ." "Withers" came back to tell me he would come himself to give me a tow in, and that I was to watch out for him and guide him in. I did not mention the two panzers, and I hoped that the arrival of the other Honey would not upset the careful relationship that had been established between us. We finished our tea a little uneasily.

I got the operator out on the turret to help me spot "Withers" when he came within the very limited range of vision. I knew that within another 10 minutes or so the chances were that he would miss us altogether. The operator gave a sudden shout and pointed to the moving smudge in the scrub about 600 yards away. It was heading diagonally away from us towards the north-west, and I got on the air quickly, talking him in like an aeroplane landing in fog. I also told him to move very slowly as I was under observation by the enemy. I did not want to put it stronger than that.

"Withers" came in gently, and was flabbergasted when I showed him the two dim panzers and the bulky tail of the long column that was disappearing in the dark. We hooked up in something like record time and set off on the long grind back to the battalion. It was not until we were safely in leaguer that we realised that our most priceless possession had been left behind—the kettle and our little store of tea.

Seventeenth Day

THE spring had now reached its full compression, and was ready to recoil violently at the release of pressure. The fluid battle had come to an end. There was to be no more scurrying to and fro across the vasty surface of the desert, crossing and recrossing our tracks half a dozen times a day, fifty times a week. The pattern was changed to the assault on static defences left as rearguards, followed by the envelopment or breakthrough and then the brief pursuit to the next defensive position.

This did not become immediately or easily apparent. There was the knowledge, always with us, that to be obliterated by a retreating 88 was no different to being obliterated by an advancing 88. The people most concerned are pretty unaware of the subtle difference between death in victory and death in defeat. If anything, the latter comes more easily. Nevertheless, it is an exhilarating feeling, and has considerable psychological advantages, to realise that you are on the winning side.

On this seventeenth day the present was still very much with us as we moved off before dawn to be on our battle position by 7 o'clock. Any thoughts we harboured of an early end to the struggle and a triumphant march to Benghazi were rudely and demonstrably shattered when the leading squadron ran slap into an anti-tank screen, and had four Honeys knocked out in exchange for one M13 and some damage to the transport which had lured them on to the guns.

I was away on the right flank, and was gratified to know of this only second-hand over the air. We sat around for several hours while our 25-pounders thundered on to the menace concealed in the sand and scrub, and the probing went on in search of a soft spot. The enemy was reacting strongly to the new developments, and his artillery all along the line running northwards from El Gubi was pounding our tank concentra-tions with a greater intensity than anything we had previously experienced. I took it as a good sign that Rommel should now hurl shells at us instead of panzers. But then, I wasn't at that moment being shelled.

At 3 o'clock in the afternoon the information came that there was a mass movement westwards of enemy M.E.T. and tanks from the Bardia area. Apparently Rommel had given up the attempt to rescue his garrisons. The big pull-out had begun.

To try and intercept this move, the armoured brigade was ordered north, and the new order of march placed 3R.T.R. on the left flank, running right across the enemy's front. It was a very noisy and unhealthy locality, and our progress was con-tinually held up by heavy bombardments and by the need for keeping an eye on the Italian tanks that were poised in a good position to swoop out on our flank—if they had wanted to.

Normally, we did not pay overmuch attention to shell-fire except when the heaviest calibre guns were in action. Apart from broken tracks and suspension, there was little damage that could be done to a tank unless a shell happened to drop slap down the turret. This did happen occasionally, with in-describable results, but it was a remote contingency which we discarded because it was so unpleasant to think about. On this afternoon, however, so many shells plastered the earth all round us that we were compelled to shift position con-stantly.

The leading formations of the brigade reached their desig-nated position, and were pushed up north against the Trigh. 'C' squadron was sent probing out to the left to try and do something about the enemy guns and to maintain closer observation.

In a state of some trepidation my troop went forward gingerly. About 1,000 yards away was a little white-washed house surrounded by a low parapet. At first I thought this was some curious mirage which would dissolve into camels in due course, but it was substantial enough and I came to the conclusion that it must be the village of El Gubi itself. Anyway, I decided that whatever O.P.s were directing the fire of the enemy guns, some of them would be in there. In between shell-bursts I was studying this building and wall carefully through my binoculars when I suddenly felt the tank buck and heard the sharp crack, either of a gun or of the impact (I could never be sure which). At the same time I got a fleeting glimpse of a puff of white smoke lifting out of the scrub from in front of the white walls. It was too fleeting for certainty, but was real enough to alarm me. I glanced swiftly down into the turret, where two anxious but otherwise undismayed faces stared back at me. Nothing seemed to be amiss in there.

Quickly I got the machine-gun trained on what I thought was the appropriate spot, explaining to the gunner that I wanted him to fire a long burst so that I could see the strike of the bullets in the sand and correct him on to the target area. At the same time I told my troop tank commanders what was going on, and that they were to engage the same area with machine-guns.

The Browning was just reaching where I wanted it when there was another sharp shudder-bang. This time I had seen the gun-flash clearly. I thought my gunner would have seen it too since his telescopic sight must have been trained right on it. "Get that bloody anti-tank gun quick," I told him. "He'll have us in a second or two if you don't."

There was no responsive burst from the Browning, and I

felt the tug on my trousers. The gunner was lying crouched in the bottom of the turret with the operator working over him with dressing and bandages. He shouted up at me: "He's got it in the leg, sir."

I told the driver to reverse out as quick as he could. Then my troop sergeant came on to tell me he had seen the flash, and that he was engaging the anti-tank gun. I told him we had been hit and that he was to pull back until he could find a hull-down position, then continue firing. Next I contacted "Withers" and asked him to arrange for medical attention at B.H.Q., where I was going to take my gunner.

I was pleased to see the other troop tanks reversing slowly as I had taught them, with both their guns blazing away. When I thought it was safe to turn about we speeded up and wheeled away back to H.Q.

It's a hell of a job getting a badly wounded man out of a tank. We extricated him as gently as we could, not without causing him a good deal of agony, through the driving compartment out of the front of the Honey and on to a stretcher which MacMillan and his orderlies had made ready.

The poor gunner had a hell of a hole in his thigh. When he had been laid on the ground in the shadow of a truck and Doc had got to work on him with the morphia and dressings I went back to inspect the damage to the Honey. The first shell —it looked like a 30-mm.—was still embedded in the front plate. A foot or so away from it there was a round pock-mark in the armour-plating ending in a small, clean hole not half-an-inch in diameter right in the middle of the driver's visor. Whaley was the first to spot what had happened. The AP shell had struck fair and square on the head of a rivet. The rivet, plus a stream of hot lead, had hurtled straight past the driver into the turret and embedded itself in the gunner's leg.

I made Whaley climb back into his seat. Then I closed the visor and peered back through the little hole. That stream of molten lead and rivet could not have missed his left ear by more than one inch.

"You ought to become a missionary, Whaley, when this is over." He stared fascinated at the little circle of light just in front of his face.

We went together over to the gunner, now full of morphia and with a cigarette between compressed lips. The doctor had his orderly make us a cup of tea each, and we sat alongside the stretcher chatting of everything except that leg. He was a good chap, that gunner, and a good gunner. I was sad at losing him.

He said to me with a tight smile: "Did I do all right, Bob?"

It's funny how many of them will ask you that—the good ones who have done all right but want to be quite sure about it, as something very important to themselves and their whole future.

"You did fine, Bill. Just hurry up and get better and come back. There's always a place for you in my tank."

"Thanks Bob. You don't mind if I call you Bob now, do you sir?"

"You can call me anything you like, Bill."

Then they took him away to the ambulance. I asked the Doctor:

"How bad is it?"

"The bone's badly smashed. I dunno . . ."

When I told him what had hit that leg he raised his eyebrows and shook his head.

"He won't lose his leg altogether, will he Doc?"

"Can't tell. He may be all right."

The gunner never came back to our Honey. They had to cut his leg off.

Eighteenth to Twentieth Day

To our great astonishment we headed our tanks towards the sunrise as soon as we woke, and rumbled straight back to our old stamping ground at Bir Berraneb. It only increased our bewilderment when the gen came round that the previous day's operations had been successful, and we were to stand-by to move to an area south-west of El Adem. There was one proviso—we would only move if all went well with the programme laid on around Gubi for the Indian Brigade and the Guards Brigade which had recently been sent forward.

Alas, all did not go well. Rommel made a vigorous counter-attack with the remnants of his two panzer divisions on the Indian infantry, who had to fall back hurriedly into the Guards' position further south. Incredibly enough, the German commander was still hanging on grimly to the idea of a decisive blow in the desert so that he could relieve his forces in Sollum and Bardia. He had, in fact, intended the attack on El Gubi to be a desperate and decisive encounter with the British armour. He could hardly imagine that at such a moment, during the pregnant afternoon of December 5, the British armour was some miles back at Berraneb practising a new method of night leaguering.

Thus Rommel's destructive blow fell on one infantry brigade, who side-stepped hurriedly and left the punch to peter out in the empty sands around the Well of Gubi. That night the Axis high command held a conference to hear an emissary of El Duce tell them that the situation in the Mediterranean was such that further shipments of anything but small quantities of men and equipment were out of the question. Rommel then revealed to General Bastico, his Italian opposite number, that the two divisions of the German Panzer Korps had started the battle with more than 250 tanks and that they were now reduced to fewer than 40.

Poor General Bastico, who had been carefully kept out of the picture all along, was dumbfounded. He quickly agreed to the withdrawal to Tripoli, and that the Agedabia line should be fortified and manned as swiftly as possible.

It was indeed a significant time in the battle, this eighteenth day, but in 4th Armoured Brigade it passed us by completely. Back at Berraneb we had no inkling of the swift climax that was approaching. Indeed, we thought the army commander's intentions were slightly optimistic. In the evening there were none of the customary orders for the following day, except that we heard an attack was to be made on El Adem.

The new style of leaguering was a great success that night, and I went along as usual to MacMillan's ambulance to have my foot seen to. Every night, when I took off my desert boot, the sock would come away in a soggy mess.

"I wish we could stop this bleeding, Bob," the Doc said. "If it doesn't stop pretty soon you'll have to go back to rear echelon to get it fixed up."

"Not bloody likely. Send me back to Alex or Cairo and I'm all for it. But I'm not going to loaf around some divisional or Corps area saluting staff officers every five seconds just to get my big toe bandaged."

He put a new dressing on and I went back to my tank to listen to the 9 o'clock B.B.C. news—10 o'clock Western Desert time.

We were bustled out of our blankets before six on the morning of December 6. It was the nineteenth day, and we had to be ready to move in half an hour—no brews. In 20 minutes we were in our Honeys with engines revving warm. The orders came through the earphones: "4th Armoured Brigade will move on a bearing of 280 degrees for 18½ miles, 3R.T.R. leading, three up."

As we lined up on the new bearing and rumbled off to the west, I measured out the distance roughly on my map. 18½ miles was going to take us well to the other side of the enemy lines. The Indians must have done all right. Nobody told us they had been driven out of their positions the previous evening. However, somebody remembered in time, and it was not yet 7 o'clock when we were told that the leg had been reduced to 10½ miles.

By 8 o'clock 'A' and 'B' Squadrons were in contact with about 30 enemy tanks, who had withdrawn rapidly.

'Eyeties,' I thought, away on the left flank. 'Why do I never get a crack at those M13s?'

With news of the contact made further north still ringing in the earphones, we pressed on cautiously, searching the ground ahead for the first tell-tale flash and puff from a hidden gun. Coming over a low ridge I was a little surprised to see a Volkswagen staff car not more than 100 yards in front of me with four Jerries attached to it . . . one at the wheel and the other four pushing like mad. My surprise was nothing to the one they got. Goodness knows what they were doing out there. They threw up their hands as soon as my Honey appeared over the ridge. We moved up alongside where their car was stuck in soft sand. I pointed to the tow rope on the side of the tank and they quickly interpreted my gesticulation. When we were hitched up the tank pulled them clear quickly and I sent them all off—there was one officer among them—to battalion headquarters, escorted by my troop corporal.

A cluster of armoured cars moved across us, and I hurried

to cut them off. It was a troop of 6th South African A.C., and they were on their way to join the rest of their unit well to the west. They told me that the previous night a German column had passed right through their lines, and that they had knocked out two tanks.

We parted with a few nostalgic Afrikaans farewells. I waited till they had got well ahead before moving on. It is a comfortable feeling to know that nothing is suddenly going to go bang at you.

In the evening, without any further incident during the course of the day and while I was wondering what had happened to the opposition, 3R.T.R. wheeled off northwards to protect a 'Jock' column (a highly mobile composite packet of infantry, field-guns and anti-tank weapons) which was anticipating an attack by enemy tanks. Once again this turned out to be a sort of crescendo effect of an accumulation of imaginations rather than fact, but it kept us out till dark, and the whole battalion got hopelessly lost on the way back. About 10 o'clock we finally leaguered where the moment found us, with an assurance from brigade that our replenishment vehicles would be sent up at first light, when they would be able to see us. The C.O. sent for me, and told me to take a troop out at dawn to make sure that we were not interfered with from the north.

Just before sunrise the next morning I was off with my other two Honeys, and within half an hour was back on the rim of the Sidi Rezegh escarpment in what had become very nearly a reserved parking place. We were directly above the landing ground, deserted now of anything live or intact, and I was listening to the inter-battalion chatter on the wireless and wondering if we could risk a brew when I suddenly spotted a small moving object coming towards the northern edge of the aerodrome. My troop sergeant was in his turret about 30 yards away, and I beckoned him over. Together we examined this solitary vehicle. It was a small armoured car, of some sort and I realised that if it continued its course it would reach the escarpment just below me. It was impossible to identify it any better than that, and I got in touch with the C.O. to ask if he could establish the position in front of me so that I could make up my mind whether this vehicle was enemy or friendly. After a minute or two he told me to assume that anything on the airfield or north of it was enemy. By this time the armoured car was half-way across the landing ground and the first rays of the sun were striking full on it. I sent the sergeant back to his tank with instructions to get his guns on to it, but not on any account to fire unless he heard me fire. Then I told my gunner to get his crosswires on target for the 37-mm.

We sat there silently, the muzzle of the cannon moving slowly downwards in conformity with the steady progress of the vehicle. Two gunners were sitting there with their fingers curved round the triggers. A gentle squeeze, and two lumps of armour-piercing lead would go hurtling through the air. That would be the end of the armoured car and its occupants. But I was filled with an awful doubt. The vehicle was beginning to look very much like one of our own scout cars. The enemy had nothing like them, but was in the habit of using all the vehicles he captured, so that was no guide. I looked in vain for the swastika and palm tree of the Afrika Korps, and then, through the binoculars, I could clearly see the two figures sitting in it. The man next to the driver wore a peaked cap, a sheepskin jerkin and a coloured scarf. It was the unmistakeable uniform of the Desert Army officer. I told my gunner quickly to unload, and got on the air to my troop sergeant and the other Honey to do the same.

By the time the scout car reached the foot of the escarpment I was standing on the edge of the cliff waving my arms to it. It came up a break in the steep slope, and soon I was shaking hands with a handsome, grey-haired officer.

"My name's Norrie," he said, and I came stiffly to attention and saluted. He was General Willoughby Norrie, commander of 30 Corps.

"Holy Smoke!" I gulped at him after I had introduced myself, "do you realise that for the last 600 yards you've been a split second away from eternity? I was told to assume that anything on the airfield was enemy."

"But the corridor's open to Tobruk. Has been since yesterday evening. I've just come from our chaps over at Ed Duda. You'd better let your people know, though it's not really important. I don't think you're going to spend any more time around this area. Well, I must be getting along. Goodbye."

He shook my hand again, climbed into his scout car and drove off to the south-east. I was considerably shaken at the thought of how near we had come to bumping off one of the most senior and ablest commanders in the British army. It would not, of course, have been my fault. It was very typical of the incredibly confused state of the Crusader battle and the complete lack of reliable information at the disposal of the fighting units.

The operator summoned me back to my Honey; the C.O. was on the air with an urgent message to rejoin the battalion immediately. As we travelled south again at full speed I heard the orders going over the air. They bore out what I had just been thinking about our information; certainly some very curious reports must have been getting back to the rear headquarters, where our future moves were planned. Once again we were given a westerly bearing to march on for 10 miles, but we hadn't gone more than 3 when the leading squadrons ran slap into a large-scale battle. It was the sort of battle we liked least—trying to get at enemy tanks lying behind a screen of concealed anti-tank guns supported by shell-fire.

Four Honeys were knocked out in as many minutes before adequate cover and protective fire could be found.

Very fortunately I was right at the tail-end of the move, having been delayed by late arrival and the need to fill up at the night's leaguer. I was soon up in the line where the battalion Honeys lay pinned down. More and more German and Italian tanks could be seen quite clearly, gathering in the distance, but every time a forward move was made the air was filled with lead and noise.

As long as we lay doggo, they did the same. We fired occasionally at long range, just to keep them nervous, and the R.H.A. plastered the whole area continuously with gunfire. I was wriggling my way forward through the convolutions of the ground, thinking of the times on the beach at Durban when I would try and get further out from the shore than anybody else, when I spotted the lorries arriving alongside the panzers and the routine movements of filling-up beginning. From the south-east a long column of transport was moving away to the north.

When I sent back this information, the brigadier laid on an attack with 22nd Armoured Brigade, but after we had watched a couple of Crusaders and a Honey go up in smoke it was called off. I couldn't help wondering whether I ought to have kept my bloody mouth shut.

By the early afternoon we had not been able to make any progress, and after the engines had been running continuously for over six hours, it was decided we needed to refill with petrol. An attempt was made to send the lorries forward to the tanks, but this brought down such a hail of H.E. and machine-gun fire that they had to run for it, and were lucky to get away all in one piece. Troop by troop we went back to replenish, returning to our forward positions as we filled up. I don't suppose any of us particularly hurried over this process. It is unbelievably relaxing to get away from the fear of sudden death, even for 10 minutes.

Reports were coming in from everywhere of continuous movement of enemy transport to the north-west, but the panzers stayed in front of us, watchful and menacing. The C.O. came on the air to say that the brigadier thought it would be a good idea for 3R.T.R. to make a demonstration against the enemy to see what effect it would have. Nobody in 3R.T.R. thought it was a good idea.

As far as I was concerned there were two tactical phrases that I had come to mistrust intensely—one was "make a demonstration" and the other was "do a reconnaisance-in-force". The ultimate intention behind both these manœuvres was to persuade the enemy to withdraw without the pressure of encounter. It usually meant that the commander wanted a success without risking casualties. This otherwise wholly laudable object very often left the junior commander right in the middle, unsupported by the discipline of direct orders and encouraged by the lack of them at the same time. It freed the senior commander of a good deal of responsibility if things went hopelessly wrong; if nothing happened the lesser man was blamed for being insufficiently aggressive, while if too much happened the luckless junior would be blamed for being over-aggressive—after a brief period of mourning.

A demonstration implied movement of some sort which the squadrons translated into a change of position, not necessarily getting any nearer to the enemy. Any interpretation of the demonstration as a move against the German armour produced an immediate and very unpleasant reaction. It was pretty tough going all along the line.

'C' Squadron was well out on the left flank, and Maegraith reported a couple of stray Mark IIIs which had come well forward from the main body of panzers and looked very much as though they were trying to get round our flank. I could think of no other reason for such a reckless move. Harry and I, with his troop sergeant, wriggled our Honeys through the sand-dunes to cut them off. We got to within about 700 yards when we saw the reason for their excursion. The two panzers had come to a halt behind some low mounds of earth which looked as though they had been recently thrown up from slit trenches. Nine or ten men jumped up and ran for the tanks.

We wasted no more time. The panzers were broadside-on, and as the first men reached them our three cannons went into action almost simultaneously. The red tracers streamed in flat lines just above the scrub, and in a few seconds there was that most satisfying of sights—a turret flapping open and figures leaping out and down. The unfortunate infantrymen stopped in their tracks and fell flat as soon as the firing started. The second Mark III spun its turret towards us, and there was one ominous orange-tinted puff of smoke from its gun muzzle before the 37-mm. shells from all three Honeys pounded into it. The enemy gun did not fire again, but nobody baled out, and we continued to pump lead until we saw the black smoke rising. In a few seconds it was a blazing inferno.

Our very natural self-satisfaction was short-lived. What seemed like every gun in the Afrika Korps and most of the Italian seemed to open up on us. We beat it out of there as fast as we could, heads well down. A couple of minutes later, behind the welcome shelter of a sandy ridge away from the tumult, I halted my driver and looked out to survey the damage. Maegraith pulled up alongside and shouted something. I took the earphones off to hear him.

"My sergeant's had it," he said, and for the first time I noticed that one Honey was missing. Carefully we moved to the top of the ridge, and from a turret-down position we looked back across the desert. Some 500 yards away the Honey lay desolate in the spurting explosions that still straddled it. Through binoculars we could see the dangling track and the shattered suspension. There was no sign of the crew, and we scanned the ground anxiously but without reward.

I got on to "Withers" to report the two tanks destroyed, as well as our own loss, and told him we would hang around a while in case any of the Honey crew had survived. We had not escaped undamaged. Water was pouring out of the cans on the back, the bedding rolls were torn to shreds and a complete pair of bogie wheels had disappeared from my tank.

Harry was shouting something, and I looked round to see him standing on the crest of the ridge waving his beret. I ran over to him and saw the figures of the missing crew running flat out through the scrub. Soon they saw us, and changed direction. Miraculously there were four of them—and unharmed. In a few minutes they were with us; breathless, slightly dazed, but overjoyed that they were still alive and in one piece. We piled them on our two tanks and took them in to battalion H.Q. where we spent the last hour of the day as the fighting died down with the dying sun.

At 6 o'clock the firing stopped, and in the growing darkness the squadrons were recalled to the rallying point. Thence we moved back 3 miles to the south-east and safe harbourage. Mine was one of 4 Honeys that had to be evacuated that night for repairs. I had another one before morning. The last news that came around before we dropped into sleep was that we were to move at dawn to Bir Belchonfus, some 10 miles south of El Gubi. We seemed to have heard all that before.

Twenty-First and
Twenty-Second Days

MOST surprisingly, after the previous day's difficulties, the brigade reached Bir Belchonfus without serious incident. 5R.T.R. went on ahead to clean up a small pocket of M13s, and the composite Crusader squadron of 22nd Armoured Brigade was sent off on some special mission. Taking advantage of the brief lull, our C.O. made a strong appeal to Gatehouse for half an hour's break so that the tank crews could have some breakfast. We had not had a meal or a brew for over 36 hours. The request was granted, and soon the emptiness of Belchonfus was a bustle of khaki figures and thin spirals of smoky fires.

By 9 o'clock we were on the move again, heading north-west well into enemy territory—or what had just been enemy territory. 3R.T.R. was now covering the west and north-west, and for some miles we passed through an area where the Guards and the Indian brigades had fought their battle. The ground was littered with the abandoned paraphernalia of war, including one lonely and mournful Matilda. Out of curiosity I had a quick climb round it, and among other personal effects found some scribbled sheets of paper. Without time to read them on the spot I thrust them into the breast pocket of my battledress and hurried on to join the rest of the squadron.

In the afternoon the leading tanks ran on to another anti-tank screen which, this time, the brigadier was content to engage with the 25-pounders. 'C' Squadron was not concerned in the afternoon's performance, and I took the opportunity to glance again at the papers I had found. It was several sheets of poetry, and had obviously been recently composed in the desert. This was one of them :

THE SHELL

The silver scream comes nearer
—faster than wind, faster than sound—
it is the song of a new-born thing,
singing her joy that she lives at last.

Her life is short, too short,
but joyous more than many million things.
She droops to die, so soon,
for now she cries no more from joy,
but in her agony of death
her scream has changed to one of fear.

She falls to earth.
And there's a breathless hush upon the land
for death is near.

For in this particle of tiny time
her fear is caught by those nearby,
and stomachs turn and fingers twitch
and then within her agony of death
she leaves the world.

She leaves it with a cry, a shout, a trumpet-call
that brings a terror to your heart,
and death flies all around.

Her grave stands open to the sky;
and there she lies together with
the shattered limbs and bleeding mouths
and eyes that nevermore shall see.

Another scribbled page was inscribed: *On Seeing Mersa Matruh Again After Five Years.* . . .

> *So many years have slowly drifted by*
> *but seeing you again below this hill*
> *Whereon I stand—I know at once that I*
> *have not forgotten you, and also still*
> *remember all your little streets that run*
> *down to the Bay, thru soft and snow-white sand;*
> *And gentle evenings when the setting sun*
> *Caressed your walls with magic hand.*
> *But in the Bay, instead of lazy craft*
> *I see—destroyers, transport ships and more;*
> *and in the streets where little children laughed*
> *tanks thunder by and shout, "To war, to war!"*
> *So close your eyes and brush away your tears,*
> *they'll come to you again—the peaceful years.**

That night in leaguer, as Doc MacMillan attended to my foot, the Colonel came over and said he wanted me to take my troop out when the leaguer broke in the morning, to make contact with the tanks of the 22nd Armoured Brigade who were leaguering several miles from our position, but whose exact location was not clear. The brigade was moving to take up a new battle position at Bir Hatiet Genadel, and the C.O. did not want to risk running into our friends in the half-light of dawn.

I moved off with two other Honeys in the first grey light. We had no great difficulty in finding the Crusaders of the City of London Yeomanry, who were still in leaguer when we reached them.

I was directed to the commanding officer, and told him

* These verses were composed by Captain Browne, Royal Tank Regiment, who was subsequently taken prisoner.

where the Brigade tanks were heading so that when he moved he would not cross their line of march. He told me he had two patrols out to the north and north-west and indicated with a sweep of his arm the direction in which he had sent them.

"Then there's nothing out this way, sir?" I asked, pointing to the north-east, towards which I would be going to rejoin my squadron on the march.

"No," he replied. "If you come across anything over that way it's not likely to be friendly."

I saluted, and left him. In the east the sky was red with the promise of day, a mist hung over the desert thickened by the dust churned up by the passing of many vehicles in the still air. Suddenly, out of this obscurity, two shapes emerged. I was, I suppose, less than two miles from the C.L.Y. leaguer. I halted the troop and stared through my binoculars . . . no identification pennants, no wireless masts, turrets clamped down, and the low, squat lines of the panzer.

We edged a little closer. There was no movement from the two tanks which had their backs towards me facing east. The nearer I got the more they looked like Mark IIIs. But I was still not sure—chiefly because the last thing I expected to see just there were two isolated panzers. But by now the unexpected was commonplace. I signalled to my other tanks to halt and stay where they were. I was going to make dead sure what those two vehicles were before attacking them. Telling Whaley to speed up, I rushed headlong towards them on a diagonal course at about 30 miles an hour. If they were Jerry and they saw me I would have plenty of speed to play with, and my course would make me a difficult target.

I kept going towards them until, with my naked eye, I could count the one, two, three, four, five, six bogie wheels. I had closed to within 200 yards and I had satisfied myself beyond doubt that they were Mark IIIs.

I watched their turrets anxiously as my Honey wheeled round behind them, but they did not swing round after me. I got on the air to my troop tanks, told them there were two Mark IIIs and they were to open fire as soon as I rejoined them. The troop corporal called back immediately to tell me that his breech block had jammed open and he could not get it clear. I ordered him back to the C.L.Y. leaguer as fast as he could go to get some assistance. Unless we were lucky enough to knock out those panzers with our first shots, I did not fancy our chances much if it came to a short-range duel.

I pulled up about 30 yards away from the troop sergeant's tank, gave him a thumbs-up sign, and then our cannons blazed out. I put four shots into the nearest Jerry, and saw the crew baling out. By this time the other one had moved off in a hurry and was jinking about the desert its turret swinging round towards me as it moved. I could see the tracers of our shells whizzing past it, and one or two went ricochetting high into the air. I saw a Crusader speeding across the desert towards us and I thought "That's fine. Now we'll get the bastard." Then I looked again, my heart coming into my mouth in sheer horror. An officer was sitting on front of the Crusader waving a red flag. I knew immediately what I had done.

"Cease fire," I yelled at my gunner, and then into the mike at the troop sergeant.

I had knocked out one of our own tanks. I jumped down and ran over to the approaching Crusader, and together we went to the shattered tank.

Three men were clustered round it. Scared and bewildered and shocked. One was holding his arm tight against his side.

There was one man short.

All the way over I kept muttering to myself: "Don't let anybody be dead. Don't let anybody be dead."

I ran to the little group. A young officer was in command. He waited for me with blanched face.

"You bloody fool. You've killed my gunner."

I hated him at that moment as much as he hated me. He wanted to hit me. I could see that. I didn't say anything. If he didn't understand how I felt, there was nothing I could say would make him.

They got a rope around the figure lying in the turret. I had neither the strength nor the will to help. Perhaps he wasn't dead. Perhaps he was just unconscious. The officer might have made a mistake. There was still a little hope.

Out of the turret-top they hauled a lad's body—red hair, fair skin, freckled face. As they pulled him out, the head rolled sideways and two, wide-open, empty eyes looked straight into mine.

In that moment I touched the rock-bottom of experience.

Somewhere behind me, from a world that I thought could never be the same again, a voice called me. I looked round and saw that they had brought my Honey over and the operator was saying "The major wants you on the set, sir."

Listlessly I climbed into the tank to hear "Withers". "Listen, Bob, I know what's happened there. It's not the first time and it won't be the last. You can't worry about that now. You've got a job to do. There's a Jerry column crossing our front. You're to rejoin immediately. Get on with it."

I said into the mike "Driver advance," and drove away without another look. Later I wrote my apologies and sent them over to the C.L.Y. But the incident would never close for me.

Many years later I met a tall young man in a Fleet Street pub, who said pleasantly : "You won't remember me, but we have met before."

"I'm afraid I can't recall . . ."

"It was one early morning in the desert. I was in a Crusader that you knocked out."

For a moment or two I was speechless, living again the horror of that morning. Then I said: "Remember you! I wish to hell I could forget you."

His next words were unexpected: "Bloody good shooting," he said, grinning broadly. "There were four holes in the turret before we could even get the engine started. You must have had a damn fine gunner."

When I rejoined the battalion the enemy column had retreated behind the usual screen of guns, and we spent a whole day watching the effects of our field-guns and spraying the area ahead of our tanks with rather hopeful machine-gun fire. At nightfall we withdrew some 4 miles to the south-east and hoped fervently that the enemy would be doing the same in the opposite direction. It was now pretty apparent to us all that Rommel was pulling out, using these delaying tactics to extricate his forces as intact as possible. It was an effective move, and obviously we were not accomplishing our rôle of destruction. It would have been folly to press an attack against those anti-tank screens. They would very soon have reduced our numerical superiority in armour.

In leaguer that night I was dispirited and miserable, a red-haired, wide-eyed ghost my constant companion. What I needed now was a lot of action. I hoped I would get it. There were possibilities in the nightly orders. We were to re-occupy our battle position at Bir Hatiet Genadel and press on to Point 161, some miles to the north-west.

Twenty-Third to
Twenty-Eighth Day

W E all thought this was going to be a hell of a day. The most nerve-racking and unpleasant form of encounter the tank man has to face is the frontal assault on a prepared position. We realised we couldn't just sit and watch all day, and we also knew that each anti-tank screen would be succeeded by another one the whole length of Rommel's retreat back along the coast. We were sustained, of course, by the thought that victory was in sight, and that the battles the enemy was making us fight were delaying efforts to enable him to get away, not battles that he hoped to win. But that did not increase our desire to die bravely for the motherland.

There was another encouraging sign. The litter of the battlefield was now all German and Italian—abandoned supply dumps and headquarters, evacuated field hospitals, broken-down transport and guns . . . all told their tale of defeat and hasty departure.

When we reached our battle position on Point 161 we were all very intrigued by the news that the C.O. had gone off to Brigade for a conference. This always foreshadowed some new development, and our guess was that we were going to be regrouped and sent on some great swan around to the west to try and get at Rommel without having to bump our heads so painfully against the obstacles he dropped off behind him.

We were quite wrong. When the C.O. got back he summoned squadron commanders, who passed on the gen to troop commanders who handed it on to their troops and so on round the whole battalion. It was incredible news—incredible because we were kept in ignorance of the overall intention; we were to stay right where we were for three or four days, and were not to move beyond a radius of 10 miles from our present position. During that time a further announcement about our future would be made.

The tension was released like a snapped bowstring. Most of us were a bit disappointed that we were not to be allowed to get on with it and get the whole thing over. It was frustrating too, to have no information about the enemy or his movements.

I took my Honey and ran restlessly about the desert. The Germans had pulled out during the night, and every now and again we stopped to inspect the empty disorder left by the retreating forces.

One forlorn tent had obviously been a casualty clearing station, and it was there I picked up my first bit of loot. For the past week or so my hips and shoulders had become daily more tender through sleeping on unyielding, often rocky, ground and even more unyielding armour-plating. When I saw a folding iron bedstead in a corner of the tent I knew it was just what I wanted. We pitched it on the back of the tank on top of the bedding rolls. For some mysterious reason it interfered considerably with wireless reception, but after giving some thought to the issues involved, I decided to keep the bed.

It was, possibly, a measure of the enemy's desperation that he now stepped up the air attack on the advancing British. There were several Stuka raids every day, and more and more of his Messerschmitts made suicidal attempts to interfere with the R.A.F.'s bombing runs. Returning to leaguer with my new-found bed we were awe-stricken spectators of a fierce dog-fight above a pack of Bostons. One Boston broke formation with smoke streaming from it. We could imagine the terror in that plane as the pilot wrestled desperately with the controls. Suddenly the plane went into a vertical dive and plummeted straight down into the sand in a holocaust of black smoke. High up in the sky the oblique rays of the sun lit up pinkly a swaying parachute and the dark blob beneath it. There was only one, and we watched it drift away to the east.

A few minutes later my operator, sitting alongside me on the turret top as we made our way slowly back to the battalion, gave a yell and pointed. Coming straight for us, not more than 50 feet above the top of the scrub, were two fighters. We did not wait to identify them, but dropped simultaneously into the bottom of the turret—to the great consternation of the gunner, who was peacefully reading a Western. He was even more bewildered a second or two later when the turret rattled like a kettle drum as the machine-gun bullets pinged against it. There was a great roaring, and through the open top we had a swift and frightening glimpse of the undersides of the two planes and their black-crossed wings as they skimmed the top of the tank.

We were annoyed about this. We considered it an unsporting gesture to introduce this new element into armoured warfare. Being attacked from the air was, in our view, the prerogative of 'B' echelons, the Royal Army Service Corps and staff cars.

By the time we had got back to Point 161 the columns of tanks were already forming up to go into close leaguer. The fact that there was to be no march back that night was a clear indication that the vicinity was pretty clear of enemy. A good deal of reorganisation had already started during the afternoon. Seven new Honeys had been delivered to 3R.T.R., and crews were coming up during the night.

That night's leaguer, with the tenseness and the fear gone from the atmosphere, was almost like being back in base depôt. We were even allowed to make a brew before last light. While we all slept, blissfully as far as I was concerned on my spring bed, a good deal of paper work must have been going on at battalion H.Q., for morning brought the news that the battalion had been reorganised in 3 squadrons of 12 tanks each and that 'C' Squadron would be commanded by Captain Crisp.

At the dawn dispersal Maegraith and I moved our Honeys out into the desert, away from the rest of the squadron, for a joint picnic breakfast. The move was inspired by the fact that Maegraith had acquired a miraculous food parcel from Australia. It had come up with the rations during the night, and it was consideration rather than greed on our part that prompted us to seek isolation in order to eat it. With a good deal of ingenuity the contents of the parcel could be persuaded to provide 8 men with a little unaccustomed luxury. It could not have been stretched beyond that number without disseminating every advantage it held for us and without destroying the intentions of the sender.

Replete with strange flavours, Harry and I were strolling aimlessly through the scrub, occasionally investigating the succulents sprouting in the sand and which seemed to bear a marked resemblance to the specimens I had once dug from the hard soil of Namaqualand for Kew Gardens, when we were startled to hear a curious throbbing noise in the air directly overhead. A few seconds earlier we had heard the quick barking of ack-ack guns, but had paid no attention. As we looked up anxiously at an empty sky the distant throbbing grew rapidly into an angry buzzing, which got louder and louder every second. Something was coming at us fast—and it was completely invisible.

Harry and I looked at each other in alarm, and without a word threw ourselves flat on our faces. There was a great thud on the earth nearby and we waited with beating hearts for the explosion to tear us apart. When nothing happened we lifted our heads cautiously to see the crews of the Honeys laughing their heads off about 50 yards away.

Peering about in some bewilderment, we saw a foot-deep indentation in the soil; lying on the edge of it was the top half of an unexploded ack-ack shell. It had come whirling and buzzing down from 10,000 feet, and had missed us by about 24 inches. I was considerably shaken by the almost personal discrimination of this episode.

"Hell, Harry! When you come to work out the mathematical chances involved, that shell was several million times closer to us than an 88 going past your left ear. The bloody stuff is certainly following me around."

Back in the Honey the adjutant came on the air to tell me that 'C' Squadron would be required to send out patrols to the north and north-west within the 10-mile limit. I sent off the three troop commanders with their tanks, and took the remaining two out myself.

Two or three miles out I got a sudden fright when I saw the solitary tank nestling in the scrub. With memories of the previous dreadful morning in the forefront of my mind I approached it gingerly until I could establish beyond doubt that it was a Crusader—an abandoned Crusader. I directed Whaley alongside and then jumped across, landing on the soft cushion of the bedding rolls which were still in place and which included a very fine-looking officer's valise, with his name and regiment painted on the canvas cover. It was a 22nd Armoured Brigade tank, but the officer's name, for reasons which will become apparent, must remain unrevealed.

Everything pointed to a very rapid departure of commander and crew. Most of their personal possessions were still stowed neatly aboard. The curious thing was that we could find nothing wrong with the vehicle, and we looked in vain for

shell holes and other evidence of sudden disaster. Whaley
finally discovered that the Crusader had run out of petrol.

There was some £20,000 worth of material lying there, and
I reported its position back to H.Q. so that it could in due
course be recovered and put in action again. Then I transferred the valise and one or two other personal items to the
Honey, thinking that the crew would appreciate getting them
back the next morning.

At 3 o'clock in the afternoon the patrols were called in,
and we returned to hear some startling news. There had been
another brigade conference, from which the C.O. had emerged
with the information that 4th Armoured Brigade was to return to the Delta in three days' time to re-organise and re-
equip for employment on another front. Our conglomerate
gasp of amazement and pleasure was quickly stifled by his
next announcement that 3R.T.R. were to take over the remaining Honeys of 8th Hussars and as many of 5R.T.R. as we
needed and stay on in the desert. Later on we would be relieved by the Royal Gloucester Hussars, who were on their
way forward.

If there had been any enemy forces within a mile of the
leaguer that night they surely would have heard the com-
munal murmur of speculation as every trooper, private and
bombardier, not to mention every subaltern and colonel, discussed the latest turn of events and made unlikely guesses
about "another front". There were certainly a great many
possibilities.

To celebrate the occasion I unrolled the very posh valise
I had found, intending to make a thick mattress of luxury on
which to spend such a significant night. Already, I have no
doubt, our minds were reaching ahead to the fleshpots of
Cairo and Alex. As I unrolled the sleeping bag a pair of neatly-
folded pyjamas fell out on to the sand. Brown silk pyjamas.
It was too much for me. I stripped naked and slid into the

cool, sumptuousness of the silk and so into careless slumber. For a few, brief hours the war was over.

In the morning, before we dispersed to our watchful stations, I wrapped up the valise and sent it by scout car to Brigade H.Q., to be forwarded to 22nd Armoured Brigade with a note to the owner explaining what I had done and expressing my gratitude at the pleasure he had unwittingly provided.

To add to the general atmosphere of half-term, the battalion office lorry arrived together with a special ration truck full of bread and fresh meat—the first for 25 days. It had only just made it, as the replenishment convoy had been dive-bombed and machine-gunned for the third time in three days. Two of the lorries had been destroyed on the way up that morning, and it speaks volumes for the high standard of evasive action reached by the vehicles' crews that only one man had been wounded. It was a strange reversal of fortunes that the tank crews should now be commiserating with the 'B' echelon troops on account of the bad time they were having.

The warm, midday air of the desert hung heavy with the odours of a variety of stews as each crew prepared its own exclusive concoction. My lot settled for steak and kidney pie without, of course, the kidney. It was still lying hot in our bellies when a warning order came that 3R.T.R. was to be ready to move at 0800 hours the next morning.

Honeys from the other two regiments continued to arrive during the afternoon, and by nightfall we were practically at full strength for the first time since we had crossed The Wire. Also during the afternoon I was becoming aware of an increasing irritation all over my stomach and around my groins. Maegraith suggested it was the result of eating too much rich food, and I was half-inclined to believe him.

I scratched vigorously without any effect, and when it

became time for me to have my foot washed and bandaged I complained to the doctor about the continuous, maddening itchiness.

"Let's have a look," he said. He took one superficial glance at my nakedness and then burst into loud laughter.

"Where did you find her?" he asked me.

"What d'you mean, where did I find her? Find who?"

"The bedouin bint you've got hold of. Don't you know what's the matter with you?"

"Of course I don't. And I don't know what's so bloody funny about it, either."

"Crabs, my dear Bob. You've got a nice little packet of crabs."

"Oh, no! How the hell..."

Suddenly I remembered. The brown silk pyjamas. I told MacMillan about them. He seemed to think it was a large joke.

"Never mind the laughter, Doc. What the devil do I do about it? Have you got anything to put on?"

"Well, what you need is some blue ointment. Unfortunately, we don't have any. I suppose somebody at the War Office did not put it down on his list of likely casualties in a desert war." And he giggled away infuriatingly.

"For Christ's sake, Doc, it's no joke. What the hell am I supposed to do? You're the bloody medical authority around here. It's your responsibility to keep the fighting man fighting fit."

"Well, you can try rubbing yourself with petrol. That might do the trick. Especially this high octane stuff. But for God's sake don't strike a match while you're doing it."

I knew I could never get him to take the thing seriously, so after a few appropriate observations on the subject of Hippocratic oaths, I went back to my tank.

As soon as it was dark I filled a small tin with petrol and hobbled out into the night. Out of sight of the leaguer I poured the petrol over my stomach and rubbed it in hard. A few seconds later I was bellowing with pain and running for the leaguer as fast as my big toe would let me, shouting for water.

The next morning, together with orders for the move, we were supplied with some rare information about the state of the campaign. I crayonned the dispositions of the opposing forces on to the talc covering my map, and relayed the gen at the first opportunity to 'C' Squadron's officers and N.C.O.'s.

The enemy had been beaten back to the Gazala line, where they were making a stand and effectively holding up the pursuing Indian Division. For two days the latter had been trying to break through, but the Afrika Korps had stood firm and, backed by the combined remnants of the panzer divisions, had inflicted heavy casualties on the attackers. The momentum of the pursuit had come to a halt.

Back at Army they had re-assessed the position in the light of Rommel's stubbornness, pigeon-holed the movement orders for 4th Armoured Brigade back to the Delta, and given new orders which involved an initial and immediate advance of 15 miles on a bearing of 256 degrees. I made a cross on my map to see where this would take us. It appeared to plonk us down in the middle of an empty and apparently useless piece of desert about half-way between Bir Hakeim and Gazala.

Obviously no decisive result could be expected just from spending a night in the open desert, and it was not difficult to perceive what the Army commander's intentions were— something a good deal more conclusive and dramatic than a 15-mile march. I studied again the yellow rings denoting the enemy positions, and our own red lines and arrows. Just a little prolongation of the red and a curve round to the north, and 4th Armoured would be directly in the rear of the Afrika Korps.

I did not tell my little conference of the probabilities. It was too sudden a change from contemplation of the delights of Shepheard's, Groppi's and the Burka to be good for morale. It wasn't doing mine any good, either.

At 9.15 we set off on our 15-mile journey at a relaxed 10 or 12 miles an hour, studying the surrounding desert purely from the point of view of the scenery and not with any special vigilance. It is comforting to know the enemy is 30 to 40 miles away. An hour and a half later we were taking up a rather unnecessary battle position, in the scheduled locality, facing west.

The fact that the C.O. had to go to Brigade H.Q. to take over while the brigadier was away at a Divisional conference was an indication that something fairly portentuous was being cooked up in the rear areas, which was much as I had anticipated.

The return of the brigadier coincided with a report from our forward reconnaissance that 50 enemy tanks were approaching our position. We prepared, rather flap-happy, to do unexpected battle—only mildly surprised at the continued ability of the enemy to find more and more panzers, well above his reputed total strength. Fortunately for the brigadier's plans a correction was soon forthcoming: "For 50 enemy tanks read 50 enemy camels."

To judge by the ensuing coming and going of colonels and scout cars and liaison officers, Gatehouse was full of potent information and intention. All that was released to us, however, was that the brigade had a little job to do, but would definitely be returning to the Delta in due course. This statement was supported by the despatch to rear areas of the dismounted 8th Hussars. I doubt whether many of us were deluded by this attempt to put a little sugar-coating on what was plainly going to be a rather bitter pill.

At this stage, influenced by the sudden change of plan or the too-sharp contrast of expectation and reality, I was becoming a little pre-occupied by unpleasant forebodings. Or it may have been the long, steady drain on resources of will and energy and courage. In my mind (and I am sure I was one of many in thinking this) the battle was over. There was only the formality of mopping-up to be endured. Having survived a period when survival was subordinate to the immediate task and duty, and when exhilaration in accomplishment had been supplanted by something near to drudgery, I could find no enthusiasm or sense of purpose in a tomorrow in which death seemed to have become causeless.

There were other factors. I had had half a dozen tanks knocked out under me, I had seen tanks alongside me turned into incandescent tombs for the men trapped inside them, I had been sprayed with lead particles and God knows how many times I had escaped death by the smallest fraction of deviation in some gunner's aim; I had passed more or less unscathed through air filled with the flying steel of shell explosions and the indiscriminate hail of machine-gun fire. I tried to console myself by thinking that each battle presented exactly the same chances of individual survival or oblitera-tion. But I felt my chances were running out; that I had used them all up.

In spite of the absence of positive information and the reassuring messages from brigade, I had little doubt that our next objective was the rear of the enemy position at Gazala, and I had a frightening certainty that I was going to be par-ticularly involved in a way that would not affect anybody else. I had been afraid often enough before, but it had always been tempered by the conviction that, whatever happened to anybody else, disaster could not come to me. "It could not happen to me." It was, in fact, the basis of most of my actions. Now, in a moment of realisation that made me very afraid, I knew I had lost my immunity.

There was nothing to be done about it. I did not let it affect

my behaviour. In the afternoon we watched with interest
another Stuka raid on the supply vehicles that had come up
with us. In this comparatively isolated spot, unprotected by
the fighter umbrella that covered the main replenishment
depôts, the dive-bombers pressed home their attacks with a
good deal more determination than they had previously displayed during the campaign. The high, terrifying whine of
those evil-looking planes, reaching a crescendo of fearsome-
ness as they plunged vertically downwards towards their
targets, took me back to the bad days in Greece.

Soon the black smoke of burning lorries was rising above
the dirt thrown up by the exploding bombs. To add to the
confusion, an ammunition lorry started to explode in cascades
of high explosive, tracers and Very lights. The firework display went on well into the night without, fortunately attract-
ing any further attention from the Luftwaffe—notoriously
ill-equipped for night operations.

I came away from the evening talk at the C.O.'s tank depressed and irritable, plagued by the blasted insects which
seemed to be thriving on their diet of high octane spirit, my
foot squelching at every step in its ooze of blood, conscious
of an unreasoning sense of doom. There had been no fresh information except that the Colonel had to report to brigade
at 7.45 the next morning.

That, I thought as I wandered through the dark lines of
tanks to my own Honey, would be when we would hear all
about it; it was all being kept carefully from us until the last
possible moment; it was certainly going to be something
pretty unpleasant.

Back at my tank I glanced at my watch and told the operator to get the B.B.C.'s 9 o'clock news. He dangled a pair
of ear-phones over the side of the turret and, as usual when
they heard the first pips, those men who were not too exhausted to move gathered round to listen to the familiar.

nostalgic voice. It was not only our sole direct link with the outside world and the rest of the war; it was very often our only source of information on the war in which we were taking part.

So we listened avidly to the communiqués and then, at the end of the Western Desert piece the suave voice said: "The immediate award of the Distinguished Service Order is announced to Lieutenant, acting Captain, R. J. Crisp, Royal Tank Regiment. Lieutenant Crisp is the former South African Test cricketer."

There was a moment of complete incomprehension at this sudden intimate announcement from thousands of miles away, and then I felt the hands clapping me on the back and heard the many congratulations. It wasn't the award that startled me as much as the circumstances surrounding our hearing it . . . the barren desert, the enemy lying in wait, and that other world of B.B.C. studios and Alvar Liddells and the top end of Regent Street. I was under no illusions as to why it had got such top-level treatment. Cricket; the English and their cricket.

I did not place a particularly high value on medals. I had seen too many curious awards. But I would have been singularly unimpressionable if I did not, in all the circumstances, find it a memorable moment. It did not do much to allay my curious feeling of impending disaster, but it altered my approach to it considerably. I suppose that's what medals are for.

More from force of habit than for any extraneous reason, we went through the routine of the dawn dispersal. We did not even contemplate an air-raid. The C.O. came back from his early morning visit to brigade, while we were cleaning the breakfast utensils in the sand, with orders to move on a bearing of 350 degrees for 12 miles. This was almost due north; and studying my map, I saw this would place us at the southern end of the Indian Division's position in front of Gazala. "My God," I thought, "they're going to use us in a frontal attack to support the infantry. We're not Matildas or Valentines. Ah, well ..."

There was a slight delay while the new arrivals, the Gloucester Hussars, took up their position on the line of march, and then we set off, reaching our destination at 11 o'clock without incident and without sight of anything except the criss-cross of many tracks in the sand.

The brigade disposed itself in three close-knit regimental groups, leaving us all more than a little puzzled at the specific order not to take up battle positions but to hold ourselves in a state of readiness. We wondered at the subtle distinction which kept us, if not in a state of readiness, at least in a state of curiosity. This was not dispelled by another summons for the C.O. to attend a conference at 2 o'clock.

He was back in half an hour, and at last the big secret came out ... "4th Armoured Brigade will move south on a bearing of 193 degrees for 21 miles to locality Bir Zeidem in preparation for move west and north to Bir Halegh el Eleba on 15/12/41." This was something; and with not much more than a mental reservation on why the hell it was necessary to travel 12 miles north in order to go 21 miles south, we headed our Honeys towards the open desert away from the embattled divisions.

By 5.30 we had completed the first part of our journey. We stayed strung out wide and open across these wide, open spaces until nightfall, when we went into close leaguer feeling more like a patrol of the Long Range Desert Group than an entire armoured brigade.

This impression was consolidated by the orders for the following morning—35 miles due west at 15 miles in the hour. I linked all these great moves into enemy country very closely with my own feelings of foreboding, but as 'C' Squadron set off at the head of this great flotilla of tanks and lorries it was impossible not to be thrilled at this deep penetration of more or less unknown territory. The last few miles were literally off my operations map, which stared blankly up at me without any of the usual ridges and wadis and escarpments.

We started at 7 o'clock. To traverse 15 miles across-country over unpredictable going in one hour means going pretty well flat-out whenever possible. As we roared across the desert, I was very conscious of the great martial array streaming along behind me and the endless, sky-filled horizon before me which never came nearer. We were all caught up in this excitement of the unknown and the exhilaration of speed, multiplied a hundred-fold by the knowledge of what we were doing and the uncertainty of the morrow when we would steal up behind the enemy's back.

Two hours later I led the way down a steep escarpment, the existence of which was not acknowledged on my map. At the bottom, after the clumsy 3-tonners had lurched their way down the slope, a halt was called for replenishment. We had come just 28 miles.

By 10 o'clock, and on the move again, I had put my map-case away. It was of no further use to me. In another half-hour the course was changed to 6 degrees and we wheeled round in a vast right-angle and headed north towards the coast—and the Afrika Korps.

Far out on our right flank a troop of armoured cars of The Royals on reconnaissance had reported being shelled while stuck in swampy ground. We pushed on a little less carefree as a result, but still fast enough to complete a leg of 32 miles in four hours. The paltry mound of earth that was Bir Halegh Eleba raised itself above the scrub ahead of us at 3 o'clock. Around it in a great square the brigade took up its battle position, with 3R.T.R. forming the northern face and 5R.T.R. and the Gloucester Hussars on east and west respectively. The square was closed by an infantry battalion, the Tower Hamlet Rifles, of whom we had never heard, and the gaps on the corners were filled by the armoured cars and Bren carriers.

It was a strange feeling, lying out there in the open, to realise that the enemy whom we had so long thought of as coming from the west now lay to the east. Information about his reaction to our move was negligible and we hoped that information about us was just as sparse.

In the late afternoon a single German recce plane had swooped overhead and then flown off northwards in a great hurry. I wondered what his report would be when he got back to base, and whether anybody would believe him. Probably not.

Then there was a call for assistance from an outlying patrol of The Royals, who reported they were being attacked by a column of 20 M.E.T. with 75-mm. guns. 'B' Squadron was sent off to investigate, and for a while we listened to the quick inter-flow of chatter between the troops and the squadron commander as they came in sight of the enemy. There was a brief, long-range engagement before the column moved over the northern skyline.

Night came down on us without any further excitement and we contracted into our leaguer formation as usual, but with a guard mounted in each tank and a screen of infantry pickets posted round the perimeter. "This," I thought to myself, "is real Injun territory."

We were given a Situation Report to pass on to the troops. It contained two items of interest . . . the Indian Division was being hard-pressed by panzer counter-attacks from the Gazala redoubt; one of our lorries, broken down on the march some miles south of the leaguer area, reported putting to flight seven Italian lorries which had come nosing around apparently to give him a helping hand. The same driver also reported seeing a large column of transport to his south moving from west to east. If these were real transport and not a herd of camels, the direction they were travelling in could only mean that the enemy was still sublimely ignorant of the presence of a brigade of British tanks in the area.

All the Honeys were very short of petrol. None of them had enough in their fuel tanks to see them through a battle if one developed in the morning. The replenishment on the march had emptied all but one or two of the accompanying petrol lorries. It was a ticklish situation. Obviously, in the conduct of any future operations, fuel was a decisive factor, and Gatehouse decided to move the whole brigade back some miles to the south at first light to connect up with 'B' echelon, which was following on in the night. One of the remaining lorries containing petrol was to be sent to 3R.T.R.

I didn't much care for this last bit of information, but thought no more about it and wandered over to Dr. Mac-Millan's staff car. He looked rather anxiously at my sodden sock as I pulled it off.

"I'm getting worried about this foot of yours, Bob. You're losing too much blood."

"It's not that that's worrying me. It's getting bloody sore."

"I ought to send you back, you know. What do you think?"

It was an opportunity. For a few minutes I tossed the thought around in my mind. The fullness of an eventful day and the tingling excitement of being right there behind the enemy lines had kept my mind free of doubts and fears. Now I could balance my premonitions against an opening for escaping from them. It was a near thing.

"Tell you what, Doc. If my foot hasn't got any better by tomorrow night, I'll go back."

"All right, then; let's leave it at that. I think it would be a wise thing to do. I'm not sure I shouldn't have made you do it before."

But it was already too late.

Orders for the next morning's move had reached 'C'
Squadron by the time I got back to my tank. There was a
supplementary order which caused a good deal of comment—
"all tanks of 'C' Squadron to be refilled with petrol from remaining stocks."

"Here we go," I thought as I spread my blankets on the now
slightly-battered bedstead and listened to the half-worried,
half-jocular chatter of the crews; "this is it."

As I stretched out, the transport sergeant came up to tell
me he was going to start filling up.

"O.K., sergeant," I said. "What about the other squadrons?"

"I've had no instructions about them. Only 'C' Squadron,
sir."

"I see. Oh, well; good night sergeant. Don't make too much
bloody row."

It seemed I had hardly got my eyes closed when I felt the
hand shaking my shoulder. I came out of sleep grunting and
cursing. I recognised an N.C.O. from the Colonel's tank.

"What the hell is it now, corporal? What's the time, anyway?"

"Sorry to wake you, sir. It's only 11 o'clock. Message
from the brigadier. You are to report at his command car at
0515 hours tomorrow, sir, with the C.O. The Colonel says
will you pick him up at 5."

"Right, Corporal. Tell your tank guard to come and wake
me at quarter to . . . Good night."

The Last Day

I FELT the rough hands shaking me and heard the urgent voice close to my ear: "Wake up, sir, wake up. It's nearly five o'clock." I climbed quickly out of sleep and the warm blankets with an immediate awareness of what I had to do. The bitter night air poured over me like a cold shower, and the rows of tanks stood out black against the stars. I stumbled over to battalion H.Q. where I found the Colonel washing in a canvas basin. When he had done I scooped up a couple of handsful and splashed them over my face. The Colonel handed me his towel, and when I was dry we walked together deep into the heart of the leaguer, where the brigade H.Q. vehicles were clustered. It was a silent walk; the C.O. knew as much about things as I did.

A young liaison officer led us to the command truck and we stepped through a blanketed doorway into the sudden light of the interior. Blinking my eyes, I saw Alec Gatehouse and his brigade major, David Silvertop, with two other officers, hunched over a map. We saluted and were greeted cheerfully by the brigadier.

Gatehouse wasted no time. Putting the tip of his pencil in the middle of a long oval crayon mark, he said:

"There's the enemy. The Indian Div. is there." (A jab with the pencil.) "They are under considerable pressure from counter attacks. We are lying here." (He pointed to a cross on the map about 30 miles west of the enemy position.) "It's our job to relieve the pressure on the Indian Div. and, if possible, bring Rommel's tanks to battle. Unfortunately the brigade's nearly out of petrol. We've got enough for a limited

operation, a reconnaissance-in-force, while the rest of us pull
back to get replenished later this morning. I have decided to
send out a small party to make a demonstration in rear of the
enemy. There will be a squadron of The Royals, your squadron
of Honeys, Bob, and a troop of anti-tank guns. One petrol
lorry will go with you. You are not to get committed to a set
battle, but you must act boldly."

He looked straight at me as he said this and I nodded briefly,
unhappily. The old reconnaissance-in-force . . . the armoured
cars for the reconnaissance, the Honeys for the force. I had a
pretty good idea what that would mean. The brigadier's voice
went on evenly :

"I can't give you any instructions about what you do when
you encounter the enemy. That's for you to decide on the
spot. It will depend on the enemy's reaction. If he attacks
you in force, David, pull back, but"—and this is where he
looked at me again—"I want you to act boldly. David will
be in command of the party and will maintain communication
with me. Any questions?"

I asked about the wireless net between the armoured cars
and my Honeys, and it was arranged to get our sets on net
while we were getting ready to go. My C.O. said he would
keep one set in the adjutant's tank on our frequency. Silvertop gave me the bearing on which we would march and the
order of march, and said we would leave at 6.30. Alec Gatehouse wished us good luck; we all saluted and left him in
the darkness as he switched off the light and opened the door.

The dark of night was going grey at the edges as we split
up and went back to our respective vehicles. I called a quick
squadron conference to tell them where we were going, and
sent all operators to their sets to get on net. The faces around
me, pale in the pale light, registered no emotion. "When we
get there," I ended, "I'll be able to tell you what we're going
to do, not before. Right; start up."

Shortly after 6 we moved out of leaguer, leaving behind our shared security and the curious clusters of tank crews from the other squadrons who had come across to see what was going on.

When we were well clear of the massed lines of tanks and vehicles, we got into position for the start on the line of march. Three troops of Honeys were in line abreast ahead of me, each troop a fairly close-knit unit moving one up. On the left were ranged the squadron of Royals, well spaced out and hardly visible in the half-light. Directly behind me stood Silvertop's armoured car, and behind him the portee trucks of the anti-tank troop and the solitary bulk of the 3-tonner.

I don't think anybody was feeling particularly happy about the prospects, but I reckoned that by comparison with the two men in that petrol lorry the rest of us were pretty well off. I shuddered to think what would happen to them if anything really started. Every gun within range would open up on them, and they would be the obvious target for any Messerschmitt or Stuka which happened to pass overhead.

I was distinctly worried about the composition of this little force. There was nothing that the armoured cars could do in the way of reconnaissance that the Honeys couldn't do equally well, and I knew that if we were attacked by panzers they would have to beat it. Nor could I foresee any possible situation, unless we were completely surrounded, in which the anti-tank guns could be properly brought into action. The petrol lorry was no doubt essential in view of the mileage ahead of us, and was an expendable risk, but both it and the trucks carrying the 2-pounders would seriously hamper progress if we had to make a run for it. I was in no doubt at all that at some stage we would have to move pretty rapidly; I also had a pretty good idea who would have to cover the withdrawal.

Promptly at 6.30 we set off in open formation. I had hoped

originally that the armoured cars would fan out ahead of the Honeys, but they stayed out on the left flank. The wireless net was as unsuccessful as I had expected it to be in those hurried circumstances. For a few minutes at the beginning of the move I was able to talk to David Silvertop and hear the armoured cars; then the whole thing went off net, and as a result we lost touch within the squadron as well. I told the operator to concentrate on getting my troops on net and never mind the armoured cars. My anticipation of the course of events did not involve instructions from the distant rear.

The sun came up red and clear straight ahead of us as we moved swiftly across an open, empty desert. The brilliance of the morning, the rare, invigorating air, and the sense of curiosity and excitement at the novel adventure, all combined to dispel my depression and dissatisfaction. In front of me the three clusters of Honeys pushed on purposefully; away on the left and in the rear the first rays of the sun made moving pink patches of the armoured cars against the dark green of the scrub still nursing the night. Behind, the trucks weaved through the rough going and the tall lorry lurched and swayed.

The sun rose higher, and still the land all round us stayed empty of movement. The rubble of Bir Temrad went past us and disappeared in the west. Then dimly, just before 10 o'clock, I saw the smudges and shapes on the eastern horizon stretching right along the perimeter of vision. At the same time the reports started coming back from the forward troops. I told them to slow down and keep a close watch on their front. `

We crawled slowly forward, and every minute the blobs and shapes grew more clearly into vehicles and guns and tanks, ranged in a long crescent line along a ridge running southward from Gazala. We were pointed right at the middle of the hollow of the crescent. Straight ahead of me, looming above the other silhouettes on the skyline, was an enormous command vehicle looking like some doubled-storeyed caravan. That, I thought, must be where Rommel is.

We sneaked up to within two miles without apparently being noticed. Then I called a halt, and tried vainly to get in touch with Silvertop to find out what next. It was a fantastic situation. We were within the horns of the crescent, we could see men moving about and the muzzles of the field-guns pointing over to the east. We just sat there waiting for something to happen, not quite believing in the enemy soldiers unconcernedly washing up their breakfast plates and going disinterestedly about their camp chores. A big Mark IV came out of the cluster of vehicles and tanks on our extreme left and cruised slowly across to the opposite tip of the German position. It passed right across the front of the three troops of Honeys, and we could clearly see the crew sitting in their shirt sleeves on top of the turret. They looked over towards us without realisation.

For another 10 minutes we sat there motionless. I looked at my watch. It was 10.15. I looked behind me and saw—a long way back—the yellow dots of armoured cars and the 3 or 4 wheeled vehicles. There was no communication with them. I got on the air to the C.O., with whom I had stayed in contact and who had ordered wireless silence in the battalion so that I could reach him at any time.

I told him what the situation was and that, as I was not in touch with Silvertop, I proposed to act on my own initiative. I asked him to pass on my remarks to David through the brigade wireless link.

The plan I had in mind was to make a charge in line abreast, straight towards the middle of the rear of the German position. When we reached it we would swing north in line ahead, and run along the whole length of the enemy lines blazing away with everything we had before wheeling out and away at full speed. It was the sort of recklessness that was, in fact, pretty safe in execution. By the time the Jerries had woken up to what was happening we would be in the middle of them, every gun firing and every tank going flat out. None of their weapons would be ready for us; they were all directed towards the east and the Indian Division. They would not be able to engage us while we were right in their own position. By the time we swung out again there would be so much consternation and confusion, and we would be going so fast, that I had every prospect of getting away with it scot-free—without losing a single tank. Personally I had my eye on the big command waggon with secret hopes of a staff conference in progress as the Browning bullets ripped through the sides. It was the sort of plan which I could not properly describe over the air, but it was essential that it should be described and timed so that each tank commander knew what to do and when to do it, so that it would function perfectly even if something happened to me. I was about to summon troop commanders to a quick conference back at my tank (it would have to be darn quick) when one of them came on the air to report four enemy tanks moving out from the left and coming across his front.

As he spoke I could pick out the panzers sauntering through the scrub. They were a good deal nearer than the one that had preceded them, and all looked like Mark IVs with perhaps one Mark III. It did not seem possible that they could pass that close without identifying us. I had to make a quick change of plan. . . .

"Hullo, BOSCO, BOSCO calling. Four enemy tanks approaching from left. Attack them when in front of your position. Do not let them get away. BOSCO to BOSCO off."

In another minute or two all the squadron Honeys were in action. There was a wild flurry of bodies on the tops of the panzers as the crews dived for turrets or fell off on to the ground. They did not try to fight it out once they realised what was happening, but fled for the opposite perimeter. Two stayed behind, still and silent.

It was, of course, the end of that peaceful morning. The flap that followed in the German lines could be clearly seen with the naked eye. Men started running in all directions; vehicles started moving, and guns were pulled into position and switched round; the big command vehicle started up and lumbered slowly and bumpily northwards and over the crest of the ridge. Then I spotted the panzers. 9 or 10 Mark IVs came down the ridge to our south, and we turned to meet them. I hoped that the armoured cars would be doing something about our rear, but I had no time to pay any attention in that direction. The panzers did not press home their attack. They sat on the forward slope beyond our effective range with the 37-mm., and lobbed shells all over us. We fired back as best we could, but our tracers made beautiful, harmless parabolas that pitched dustily in the sand or made wild riccochets as they bounced off armour plating.

It was not the sort of situation that could be continued indefinitely. I reckoned we had fulfilled everything that anybody could extract from "reconnaissance-in-force". As far as I could see, none of the Honeys had suffered any damage, but I knew that those Mark IV gunners, unlike field gunners, would be aiming directly at our tanks with their H.E. and inevitably hits would be scored. Our immediate safety lay in dispersal, and I was worried when I saw two Honeys almost touching each other, firing away like mad. I had already given the order to start pulling out when through the earphones came :

"Hullo, BOSCO. BOSCO Two calling. We've been hit and can't move. We're baling out. Two to BOSCO, over."

"BOSCO. O.K. Bale out and get on that Honey alongside. We're pulling back now. BOSCO, off."

I was watching them closely from about 100 yards away, and to my great relief saw their tank reversing slowly and then move forward and wheel away. It happened fairly often that drivers and commanders, after their tank had taken a direct hit, leapt to the conclusion that they were immobile. Then I saw the explosion right under the front of the second Honey and, as the dust and smoke cleared, there was the track sagging limply. The tank gave a few abortive jerks as the track flailed round the driving sprocket and then the crew started to clamber out—commander, operator, gunner from the turret, driver from his little opening in front. To my dismay I saw it was Harry Maegraith.

They grouped together at the back of their Honey, ducking at each burst of H.E. which was falling thickly all round us. I noticed that the other troops were moving back westwards, and I waved to Harry and his crew, at the same time directing my driver towards them.

They left the shelter of their tank as they saw me coming, and ran towards me. Every now and again one of them would fall flat, and I thought "He's had it"; then he would get up and keep on running and I could not help smiling as I realised that what was making them fall was nothing but jelly knees. They all reached the Honey miraculously unhurt, and clambered up on the back. I leaned over to make sure they were all on.

"O.K., Harry?"

"O.K., Bob."

Still leaning over the back of the turret I put the mike to my lips and said, "Driver advance. Hard left." I had the mike to my mouth when I heard the enormous crack right next to my head. In the same split second I felt my knees buckling under me and the darkness falling upon me.

There was no pain; just a numbing shock and a feeling of

great astonishment. I knew immediately that I had been hit in the head. I felt myself sliding down to the bottom of the turret. On the way down and out I had only one thought in my mind, and I wrestled with it savagely. I had given the order "Driver advance, hard left". If I didn't add the necessary word "Steady" to straighten him out on the right course we would keep on going round and round in circles on the same spot for ever.

It became an obsession. I had to say "steady". The microphone was still in my hand. With a supreme effort I got it near to my mouth. The word was there in my mind and I forced it on to my tongue. I could feel it there, a solid word. But I could not push it out of my lips. Then I felt the mike being taken from my hand and heard dimly my operator's voice saying something to the driver. It was all right. There was no need to struggle any more.

I was down on the floor of the turret, my legs crumpled untidily beneath me. The gunner was fussing about my head with some shell dressings. He was wasting his time. I could feel life slipping away from me. I knew, beyond a shadow of doubt, that I was going to die. The darkness I was sinking into was the darkness of the grave. I waited for the big experience. Death was the biggest experience in life. Everybody knew that. It was not something that people looked forward to. I was afraid of death, yet here I was dying, ready to be frightened, bewildered, overjoyed, dismayed. I waited quite deliberately for something to happen. I did not know whether it would be a vision of hell or shining immortality. Strangest of all, I didn't care a damn. Nothing happened. I waited, and nothing happened. The blackness grew deeper round me and at the edges a dark red light glowed. It was a clear impression. But as I went out into eternal darkness the last thought I had was . . . death is easy.

I did not die. A long time after—I did not know how long—
I heard the tank noises and opened my eyes. I saw the gunner's face, and the relief on it as he saw that I was back from
unconsciousness. Behind him I could see the khaki-clad legs
going up to the bright ring of light of the open turret. Then
the pain started. Somewhere round my left ear and, worse
still, my legs.

I tried a word or two hesitantly. The sound came out and
the gunner bent his ear near my mouth.

"What's happening?"

"Everything's all right, sir. We're on our way back. We've
asked for an M.O. to be sent out to meet us."

"Mr. Maegraith and the others?"

"They're O.K., sir. All on the back of the tank. Captain
Joly's taken over the squadron."

"What's the time?"

"Nearly 2 o'clock."

"Where are we? Are we near brigade?"

"We're on our way back. There's no sign of the enemy now.
We think they pulled out along the coast road. The C.O. says
the brigadier is sending out an M.O. with an armoured car
escort. They should be here any minute now, sir. Don't you
worry. You'll be all right."

He held my head cradled in his arms. Every now and again
he changed the shell dressing and I would feel the warm trickle
running over my shoulder and down my back.

Time and the tank rolled on, and I could hear the operator's voice distantly in terse sentences on the wireless. Pain
worked its way up from my legs and down from my head
until it engulfed my whole body. I longed for unconsciousness. Now that I knew that I was not going to die or, at least
that I had a chance of living if I could get some proper attention soon enough, life was once more a precious thing. But I
remembered the sensation of death and its nothingness. The

thought of it no longer alarmed me, nor ever would again. As I lay crumpled in the bottom of the tank I knew only that pain was real.

"Try and move me a little," I begged the gunner. "My legs..."

I felt him trying to lift me and struggled mentally to help him. There was no response from my muscles; not even an illusion of movement.

"Where's that bloody M.O.? Can't they hurry him up? Tell the C.O. I can't go on much longer."

The message went up to the operator and out over the air. Poor gunner. I could feel his sympathy and desperation as the long afternoon wore on. Once we stopped, and I heard the voices outside the tank and thought "Thank God. They're here at last." But it was the petrol lorry pulling up alongside to refill. We rumbled on, and the sky through the turret grew pink and then dark above me. In the bottom of the tank I tried desperately not to give way to despair, not to sound too pathetic. The left side of my head felt like hot metal poured on raw flesh, and from the waist down I was slumped in a pool of pain which I knew would stop if I could only crawl out of it.

At last I heard the operator shout down into the turret. "We can see the brigade, sir. We'll be there in two minutes." It was just after 5 o'clock.

The Honey came to a stop, and as the engine switched off I heard the voices outside and recognised Doc MacMillan's. Whaley turned round in his little compartment and said, "You'll be O.K. now, sir," and I saw the operator's legs disappearing above me to be replaced by the rosy face of the doctor.

"For God's sake get me out of here, Doc."

He looked at me speculatively for a moment or two, went

"Hmmmm . . ." and said to somebody outside: "We'll have to take him out through the front."

Somehow they shovelled me out through the driver's compartment and the front flap on to the ready stretcher. As they prized my legs out straight the relief was so immediate and so intense that I almost forgot the wound in my head. But the flame of it started as I put my head back on the pillow, and I twitched on to my side.

"Hell's bells, Mac, it feels as though my bloody ear's been torn off."

Macmillan lifted up the first-aid dressing and took a quick look. "That," he said briefly, "is the least of your troubles."

They took me to an ambulance, where I spent the worst night of my life. I got a clear impression from each of the visitors who came to see me that I was not expected to survive it. The Colonel came in to tell me that Division were arranging to have an aeroplane laid on to take me back to the Delta first thing in the morning (the staff at Divisional H.Q. actually did try to fix this, but without success). He also told me that a wireless message had been intercepted from the headquarters of the Afrika Korps saying that they were evacuating the Gazala position, and how lucky they were to escape "the steel trap". It was some compensation. I asked the Doctor about Harry Maegraith. . . .

"He's all right. Don't you worry about him."

I knew he was lying, but did not press the point. Harry would have been along to see me if he had been able to. I did not want to make sure about it. Long, long afterwards I found out that they buried him the next morning in the cool sand of the desert. He had been killed instantaneously by the same shell that had hit me.

The Days After

D R. MACMILLAN looked quite surprised when he opened the door of the ambulance in the morning and saw me looking at him more or less intelligently.

"I'm afraid they can't raise a plane for you, Bob. The 'B' echelon convoy is going back in a few minutes, and the ambulance will take you to the nearest Casualty Clearing Station. They'll fix you up there, if you survive the journey. How are you feeling?"

"How d'you think?" I said.

I was in a hell of a mess, but I was far from dead. One trouble was that the only position that did not give me acute discomfort was sitting up. I could not lie on my back or the left side because of the wound in my head. I could not lie on my right side because, for some reason, my right hip was extremely painful (I had broken a bone in my hip). When I did sit up I felt sick, and each time I got sick it was as though my brains were being squeezed slowly through my skull.

I had no idea of the extent of the damage to my head; nor did anybody tell me. My left ear felt like a miniature furnace, but the doctor had made it clear that compared with the rest of it my ear was pretty insignificant. I agreed with Mac on one point—if anything was going to kill me it would be that 50-mile cross-country ride in the ambulance. At this stage I was more or less resigned to anything that could happen to me . . . just as long as it was something other than lying there motionless.

Outside, the Honeys started up and the roar of the nearest radials swelled into a crescendo of noise as all the tanks in the brigade warmed up before breaking leaguer. Voices came back to me from the driving cab of the ambulance, and I heard the engine start and felt the gentle vibration of the engine. An R.A.M.C. orderly—who had shared the night with me, poor chap—came in and tucked me up. The C.O. and a couple of other officers stood with the doctor to say goodbye to me, the door slammed and a second or two later the long lurching, swaying, bone-jarring journey began.

I was half in and half out of consciousness, but never far enough out to be beyond pain or awareness of the jerky, swaying world which enclosed me. The sides of the vehicle grew warm and I saw in my mind the sun rising bright in the heavens, pouring its light down on interminable miles of sand and scrub and the steep-descending wadis which seemed to tilt my intestines into my throbbing skull.

Once the convoy stopped for a break. I banged on the tin between me and the driving cab, very much aware of the fact that it was about 30 hours since I had last emptied my bladder. The orderly came round to the back door.

"A bottle, please."

Half-way through this performance the convoy moved off again, dragging the ambulance with it. Jesus, I was cross about that. I swore violently at the unfortunate orderly who explained sympathetically:

"We daren't get left behind, sir. We don't know the way back on our own."

On and on, into the day and the desert. On and on . . . fast and vibrating over the good patches, low-geared and swaying through the wadis and escarpments, screaming and sliding through the soft sand. This is unending, I thought, and consoled myself with the worse agony of the long day before.

There was another halt, and this time I heard the many voices outside. The door opened and a number of men stood curious but efficiently ready to attend to me. They carried me over to a large, clean, white-painted vehicle and slid me gently off the stretcher on to a table which was all too familiar under the big light immediately overhead.

While a couple of orderlies fussed over the bandages an R.A.M.C. major came in and greeted me pleasantly. They stripped off my gory battle-dress and other clothing and put me in clean pyjamas. I felt a lot better. The officer had a quick look at the back of my head and asked:

"Would you like a drink while we're getting things ready? It'll be a few minutes yet."

I misunderstood him completely.

"I'd like a large whisky, please."

They all laughed. The major hastened to explain that much as he would like to join me in a large whisky, it was not quite the best preparation for either of us for a rather delicate operation. What he really meant was would I like a cup of tea, or some bovril?

I settled for a mug of tea and they propped me up to drink it. The doctor's name was Keller, and he was a little concerned about the imminent operation because, he told me, he was really a gynæcologist and although he knew a good deal about extracting babies, he had not the same amount of experience at extracting pieces of lead from skulls.

(I hope that somewhere Doctor Keller will discover from this that he is pretty good at extracting lead.)

"Have I got a piece of lead in my head?" I asked him. It was news to me.

"Can't think why you're here at all. It must be just about touching your brain as far as I can see," he added cheerfully.

I finished the tea and as I turned painfully over on to my stomach the doctor explained that I was too weak to have a general anæsthetic, he would have to operate under a local.

"It'll be a bit tender, corporal," I heard him say. "Better shave him after the injection."

I felt the needle going into various places on the back of
my scalp....

"Can you feel that, Crisp?"

"No, not a thing."

"Right. Get him cleaned up Corporal, then we'll make a
start."

A minute or two later the operation began. I never knew
before that operations were such chatty occasions.

"Let's have those instruments out, Bill."

An orderly dipped into the sterilising cabinet and pulled
out a succession of bright, sharp things which he laid in a
gleaming, terrifying row just in front of my face. The doctor
was invisible, but a potent presence with his voice right in my
ear.

"That should be enough hair off, Corporal. Clean it up a
bit and then we can begin. . . . We won't need the saw, Bill,
and I hope to hell the drill won't be necessary. We'll incise
first with the scalpel."

My relief at the first part of this monologue, coming muffled
through the gauze mask, was quickly dissipated by the sight
of a razor-edged gleam passing right across my eyes. The sweat
began to bead on my forehead. There was nothing to feel
beyond an awareness of pressure, but the noise in my ear as
metal went through skin and flesh was as deafening as opening a tight-fitting matchbox through a loudspeaker.

"That's about enough," the low, confidential monotone
went on. "Now we'll just retract back the scalp a bit so that
we can get at it . . . so. Hmmmm. You don't know how lucky
you've been, old boy. Good thick bit of skull here. Anywhere
else it would have been curtains. Came to rest in the dura.
The bradawl, Bill, and then the burr. No, not that one, that's
too big . . . that's the one. Now that hammer thing."

I did not see this lot going by overhead. My eyes were shut
tight and little rivulets of sweat coursed over them collecting

in pools in the hollows. Presently my skull boomed with a noise like the tom-toms of doom. I did not need eyes to see the chisel being tapped gently but firmly down into my brain. Some muscles in my neck and left leg started twitching.

"Can you feel that?"

"No. But I know what you're doing."

"That's all right. We needn't do any more of it. Soon be over now. The nibbling forceps, Bill."

I forced my eyes open just in time to see a horrifying instrument pass into the disembodied hand just above my face. There was a noise like a bad and prolonged gear-change. Then the voice said: "Better hold his head steady, Bill. Can't risk a jerk now. Can you feel anything, old man?"

"No," I said, a little reluctantly. The sweat stung my eyes as I tried to shut out the narrow world that pressed down on me so terrifyingly. Firm hands closed round my head and I was grateful for them. There was a quick moment of unretained pain and then the voice again ...

"That's got it. All over, old man. It's out. Just clean up a bit, Corporal. Dry dressing. Should plug that up with a bit of beeswax, but we have no beeswax. Here you are, old man. Show it to your grandchildren sometime, or put it in the Cape Town museum."

I saw the smiles round the room as I opened my eyes and felt the taut muscles relaxing all along my body. The doctor held out his hand to me with a jagged piece of maroon and rust-stained lead in it, about the size of one of those large "alley" marbles.

"We'll put it in your battle-dress pocket for you," he said. "Now, if there's anything you'd like, anything you fancy, we'll try and get it for you. Except a large Scotch, which is what I'm going to have."

"There is something, as a matter of fact, Doc. . . . Have you got anything for crabs?"

There was a moment of puzzled incredulity, then they roared with laughter as I told them the story. The doctor shook his head at the end of it.

"It doesn't seem to be on the list of battle casualties. Have you tried petrol?"

"Petrol! I feel I ought to go round with a sign: No Naked Lights; No Smoking. High octane, at that."

They put me back in an ambulance that would take me on to the hospital at Tobruk early the following morning. The effect of the anæsthetic wore off in about half an hour, and now that I knew what it was and where it was the pain was worse than it had ever been before. I was grateful for the morphia that lulled me softly through the long night.

Tobruk Hospital at that time was a Florence Nightingale shambles. The first 24 hours I spent on the only available space—the hard stone floor between a couple of beds. The long ward was packed with wounded, many of them lying, like myself, on the floor waiting for vacancies. When the man in the bed above me died they carried him out, picked me up, and dumped me into blankets still warm from the warm corpse.

In the morning a couple of senior R.A.M.C. officers came round inspecting the torn flesh and shattered bones. They reached me and looked briefly under the bandages. The elder man said:

"Have him X-rayed and then get a tube in that hole to drain it." He patted me on the shoulder. "With a bit of luck we'll keep you going till you reach the Delta. There's a hospital ship sailing tomorrow for Alex."

They passed on while an orderly asked my name and number and jotted down his instructions. Straight opposite me a boy of 19 or 20, his head swathed in bandages, stared at the doctors with the dark, uncomprehending eyes of a lost dog.

By the time they had reached him he was dead. They paused briefly to lift an eyelid, then the stretcher came in and the process went on as relentlessly as a car production line.

A long, recumbent queue stretched outside the X-ray room. A couple of sergeants inside went through their routine with a mechanical ruthlessness that left me cursing them with every swear word I could remember as they mauled my head about to get the right angle on the plate. I thought bitterly: "Wot-the-hell . . . general, major, private; a near-corpse has no rank, no personality, no emotions that can ever be recognised or remembered."

Back in the ward, a new lot of men lay on the floor waiting for the vacant body that would mean a vacant bed. The heavy-loaded stretchers came in and the heavy-loaded stretchers went out—carefully feet first.

At night the bombers came, heralded by wailing sirens, the sharp barking of Bofors guns and the deeper baying of heavy ack-ack. We lay and waited, shivering, for the next noise. I found my mind murmuring: "Please God, not on the ward. Please God, not on the ward." And knew that, finally, my battered nerve was broken.

A man leapt up from his bed at the far end and went down the middle of the ward cursing and shouting, his arms flailing wildly at the hostile forms that surrounded him.

Voices yelled for the orderly. A young man came in, brusque and a little bored. He took one look and ran. In a few seconds he was back with three other men. They poured all over the soldier, still fighting his wild invisible enemies. He was clamped down and fastened up, and thus they carried him out into the night.

Men muttered and groaned in the unquiet dark; from the bed alongside me a horrible rattling noise came with deadly monotony; every few minutes a match would flare in the gloom and a drawn, pain-filled face would stand out stark and hellish in a momentary incandescence. The world was full of pain and fear and hope and the oozing smell of death.

There is a long gap in my memory after the nightmare of Tobruk. Morphia clouded my day and brought peace to my nights. I remember the quayside in the glad sun and the fresh, sea-rippled breeze. Then days and nights of movement, ships and trains, ambulances, stretchers, red crosses and the broad, battle-dressed backs of the bearers looming eternally above my feet—each one identical, each one a different man, impersonal, a part of the wood and fibre of the stretcher. . . . The base hospital between Fayid and Geneifa on the edge of the Great Bitter Lake in which the narrow waters of the Suez Canal lose for a little while their close confinement. There were women there, women dressed as nurses, untouchable and almost intangible, their minds on the vigorous, healthy young Fleet Air Arm pilots nearby . . . noisy convalescents in the next ward whom I shouted at viciously when their rowdiness came to me on sound-waves that jarred my skull . . . the big male-nurse who finally produced the blue ointment that rid me of those pyjama souvenirs. . . . Professor Smith, the Edinburgh specialist, who could not quite comprehend my complaint that my big toe was hurting me. Possibly he thought it had something to do with a curious corner of my brain that had gone amiss.

I owe my life to the surgical skill of Professor Smith, but so far as I was concerned he was an uncertain psychologist. When I am ill I like to be left alone; I don't want to see anybody. He came in one day and gave me a hell of a choking off for not trying to live. "You've got to fight it," he told me roughly. "Show some guts. You're giving in to it. We can't keep you alive if you're not going to help us."

Nothing was further from my mind than dying. It never entered my head. I knew he was only trying to prod me out of a moroseness that he mistook for surrender, but it annoyed me. I glared back at him.

"Oh, for Christ's sake shut up and leave me alone."

As the infection spread under my scalp, jabbing spear-points pierced and released what seemed to be the quintessence of pain so that I would give sudden, unpremeditated yells. One day, with my temperature soaring and my head a flaming inferno, the professor came in to tell me that the mastoid was badly infected and would need an immediate operation.

They wheeled me into the operating theatre the same night. Just before the anæsthetic mask was slipped over my face, the theatre sister came to the head of the operating table with a notebook and pencil in her hand. She bent down close to my mouth.

"You'd better give me," she said in a low voice full of compassion, "the name and address of your next of kin."